Praise for The Gus Chronicles II

"For those of us who work in residential care, it's a rare opportunity to read something that speaks in real and practical terms to the reality of our almost impossible jobs. Using the literary device of a precocious adolescent, Charlie Appelstein examines the world of troubled children—friendship, rejection, drugs, and sex—while focusing on issues specific to residential treatment—restraint and seclusion, touching policies, outcomes, staff structure, and cost. He does so with great pathos and connection to the human spirit. This book is invaluable training for line workers, clinicians, administrators, and policymakers who seek to understand the world of troubled youth from the inside out."

Robert E. Lieberman, M.A., LPC
President
American Association of Children's Residential Centers

"In *The Gus Chronicles II,* Charlie Appelstein has again found a way to convey to readers that in order to help youth in out-of-home placements one must understand the ramifications of abuse and neglect, family upheaval, and what it means to live in a residential setting from a kid's perspective. This powerful book evokes laughter and tears, and places the reader squarely in the shoes of at-risk kids who have been removed from their homes."

Dave Pelzer
Author of *A Child Called It* and *The Lost Boy*

"He's baaaack...But unlike Freddie Krueger, the staple character of horror films who we couldn't get rid of, this is a very good thing in the case of Gus. We can't possibly get enough of him.

In *The Gus Chronicles II,* Charlie Appelstein brings this infectious little guy and his unique perspectives back to life. At once cynical and hopeful, selfish and sensitive, sad and funny, Gus brings the life and energy of real kids into our world. He helps us see that objectivity and detachment will never substitute for the understanding achieved through active engagement, familiarity, and a real relationship with an energetic youth. This is an especially effective approach for the direct care worker.

Charlie fills an important void in childcare literature with life and humor. I hope Gus lives on forever!"

Earl N. Stuck
Associate Vice President
Child Welfare League of America

"I loved reading each chapter; I learned something. I felt like I wanted to be better at helping kids. I laughed, I cried, and I felt very fortunate to have Gus in my life.

This book reminded me of the raw painful emotions experienced by our kids in residential treatment and other social services, of the resiliency and strength of the human spirit, how much kids need adults to be there for them, and how lucky we adults are to have children in our lives. This book leaves me with the thought that children are the symbol God has placed in the world to remind us that there is hope for a better and brighter future.

And I'm thinking this Keyon kid might be the hope for the Bears."

Jim Parcel, M.A., LMHC
Licensed Mental Health Counselor

"These stories of the struggles and triumphs of troubled kids provide insight and inspiration to all who deeply care about children in conflict."

Larry Brendtro
President
Reclaiming Children and Youth

"It doesn't have lift-the-flaps, so I don't think it will be much fun."

Julie Appelstein
Age two

The Gus Chronicles II

Also by Charles D. Appelstein:

The Gus Chronicles: Reflections from an Abused Kid
No Such Thing As a Bad Kid: Understanding and
Responding to the Challenging Behavior of Troubled
Children and Youth

Rhode Island Council of Resource Providers for Children, Youth, and Families

RICORP is a highly proactive state association. Amongst other services, the Council provides legislative advocacy, staff development programs, ensures additional clinical services for youth in agencies with limited budgets, and collaborates with other associations and State Departments to benefit children in care, and their families. Some of our programs include:

- *Psychiatric Response Network (PRN) Program*
- *John H. Chafee Life Skills Center for Adolescents*
- *RICORP Certification Training Program for Residential Staff*
- *CCRI "Children's Residential Programming" Certificate/Associates Degree*
- *RICORP Annual Conference and other professional symposiums*
- *Suitcases For Kids Program*

For more information on RICORP, please visit our website at www.ricorp.net

The Gus Chronicles II

Reflections from a Kid Who
Has Been Abused

Charles D. Appelstein, M.S.W.
(and Gus E. Studelmeyer)

Second Edition

RICORP
Cranston, Rhode Island

Published by: **RICORP**
1 Harry Street
Cranston, Rhode Island 02907

Edited by Amy Robinson
Book design by Cheryl Appelstein
Cover design by Alphagraphics

Printed in the United States of America

ISBN 0-9719640-1-7

This book is dedicated to one and to all.

The "one" is my wife Cheryl. It might sound corny, but she is indeed the *wind beneath my wings*.

The "all" is the kids I've worked with over the years. Each one has touched and taught me. It has been a terrific privilege to be a part of their lives.

Acknowledgments

Gus II might not have been written if Jim Harris and RICORP hadn't supported the project. I can't thank Jim, Betsy Bogardus Ison, and their fellow board members enough for believing in Gus.

Amy Robinson is a Boston-based freelance writer and editor who sat across from me in sixth grade. I thought she was the smartest kid in the class (although she denies it). Amy did a marvelous job editing this book. Now I'm the smart one.

Two years ago, I began writing *Gus II*. After composing the first fifty pages, I asked colleagues to read what I had written. Most thought it was excellent. But not Ol' Ernie Campagnone, the grizzled, childcare veteran from Rhode Island. He thought it stunk and said "It doesn't sound like Gus. It's too tame." Ernie was right. I erased all fifty pages and started over again. Thanks, Ernie.

Jim Parcel works with troubled kids in Iowa. He is what you call "good people." His ongoing encouragement during the writing of this book was invaluable.

Ellen Kleiner is a book wizard. Once again, her technical skills saved the day.

Gil Peters loves to play golf. But he is much better dealing with folks at risk than he is a golf ball. He provided significant technical and editorial assistance throughout the writing of this book. Gil, your approach shot to life is fantastic!

Writing this book entailed spending a number of days away from home. It was hard being away from my amazing wife and adorable daughter. Please understand that you two were never farther than my heart. I love you both.

Contents

Foreword

The *Rhode Island Council of Resource Providers for Children, Youth, and Families* (RICORP) is pleased to publish *The Gus Chronicles II* by Charles D. Appelstein. It is most fitting that this book should be our first publication.

In 1994, Charlie introduced us to Gus, a kid in residential placement who gave us insight into treatment from a child's perspective. This second look into Gus's world not only challenges professionals to continue to look at residential care from a client's perspective, but also focuses on the ever-changing landscape in our field. *Gus II* encourages us to respond to the obstacles we face in our profession.

Back in the early 1990s, when I was still a direct care worker, Charlie Appelstein was conducting a workshop at our program. As part of the training, the group read a portion of his first book, *The Gus Chronicles*. I remember the story being not only unique but right on target regarding life within the milieu. I thought, "This is one trainer who knows what he's doing. He vindicates what I feel, knows what it's like in the trenches, and can really motivate a worker." Even today, people who participate in any of Charlie's sessions or read *The Gus Chronicles* express these same sentiments. His work keeps up with the changing times: the shrinking budgets, pressure from our states to produce more timely outcomes with children, and the lack of understanding we struggle with from those outside our profession. In spite of the challenges we face, we must strive to go forward.

In *Gus II* Charlie provides additional tools to assist us in helping the youth in our charge. In this book, Gus, having entered adolescence, continues to alert us to what placement is like from a resident's point of reference. Gus is aware of the external forces that are stressing his program, including the most obvious: high staff turnover rates. Conceding the degree of difficulty residential care workers face, he still implores us not to give up on the kids in our care. If the staff at Highland Hills gives up, who is left to advocate for Gus and his peers?

In *Gus II* Charlie is (once again) doing what he does best. He empathizes with the difficult jobs direct care workers, clinicians, and administrators face. He gets down in the trenches, encouraging us to keep on giving of ourselves. Charlie knows that the role of primary caretakers of children in placement is the most important of any in a program. This book "comes through" for these folks, giving them support, motivation, and fresh ideas.

In addition to providing these things for staff, *Gus II* strongly conveys the importance of teamwork among professionals in our field. It is vital that entire teams, including care workers and clinicians, work together to develop and successfully implement effective treatment plans. Charlie knows the importance of this collaboration, and Gus acknowledges that it is vital in a child's treatment. In this day and age, the concept of teamwork is as important as any!

It was once said that the greatest thing a person can give, aside from their love, is their labor. Charlie (and Gus) knows that professionals from residential programs give both. And when we search for victories in our work, the greatest accolade we can receive is seeing a child move forward. Those outside of the field may not appreciate the magnitude of this feat, but we know it is the greatest achievement we can hope for. It is why we do our job. It is why kids like Gus keep us doing what we do best - they need us!

James R. Harris Jr., M.A.
Executive Director
RICORP
Author, *Respecting Residential Work With Children*

Introduction

Five friggin' years. Five friggin' years! That's how long it's been since I was created and asked to write *The Gus Chronicles: Reflections from an Abused Kid.* Last time I wrote a sentence Forest Gump was the toast of the town and everyone was doing the Macarena (ooh...da Macarena). Appelstein, why did you wait so long? I've had things to say. What's wrong with you, man? Well, *I guess stupid is as stupid does, Chuck!*

(*Author's note: I still hate when he calls me Chuck!*)

For those of you who didn't read my first book, let me fill you in. I'm Gus E. Studelmeyer (The E. stands for Elvis; my mother had the hots for him). In *Gus I*, I was a fictitious thirteen-year-old living at the Highland Hills Residential Treatment Center.

I have red hair, freckles, a somewhat bulging waistline, and a pretty sad history of abuse and neglect. Prior to entering residential care, I sampled a number of foster homes. As the book ended, Big Mama (i.e. my mother) was cleaning up her act and I could see a discharge date looming in the future. I was feeling nervous but hopeful.

Oh yeah, almost forgot: I have an IQ of 163...that's genius territory, my friends. I was endowed with great intellect so that I could articulate some pretty important insights.

Kinda funny, ain't it? Gump and I both came out the same year. He was a dope and I was a genius. Yet it wasn't ol' Gus that made the big bucks. I hate the jerk. I actually bumped into him last year. We fictional characters occasionally hang out. Gump whipped my ass in Ping-Pong. But then we sat down and watched Jeopardy. I knew all the answers. Gump kept saying, *"When do they spin the wheel, Gus?"* What a geek!

Hey, I'm just blowing smoke. I actually like Forest. The guy has courage. I really shouldn't be dissin' him. I know how it feels to be put down – it hurts. I guess I'm just a little jealous of the guy. Kids like me are often jealous of others...particularly those who are better off (and who's not?). It's part of the territory.

So that's who I was five years ago. Who am I today?

The same exact kid, except I'm a year older, a wee bit chubbier, have a few nubs on my chin, and I've got a ring through my ear. It turns out five years of human life is equal to one Gus year (it's kind of like the dog thing in reverse). So that's where I'm at. I'm fourteen, my hormones are jumpin' through my skin, I'm counting new pubic hairs every day, and in four or five months I'll be leaving Highland Hills for good. Gus is going home. Man, am I scared.

One final note of interest before I get going:

I refused to write this book unless the author changed the subtitle. He wasn't happy about the idea. "It will be confusing to people," he moaned. "What's wrong with *Reflections from an Abused Kid*?"

"You know what's wrong with it," I told him. "I suffered abuse, but I'm not an 'abused kid.' That's not how I choose to be defined. I'm a kid who: Loves anchovies on his pizza; flunked home-economics last semester but got an 'A' in advanced calculus; develops web pages at school; has an outrageous, yet perverse sense of humor; has won 43 games of chess in a row; hides an outie bellybutton; possesses a mad crush on

Mary Egan; and loves horror movies and Bare Naked Ladies (the group, as well). This is who I am, brother.

"Sure, I'm also a kid who was abused: A kid who has trouble fallin' asleep at night and is afraid of the dark; a kid who doesn't have many friends; a kid who suffers frequent nightmares about bad men doing bad things to him; a kid who suffers painful pangs of hopelessness; a kid who has cut himself; and a dude with a lot of rage inside.

"But don't label me an abused kid. It implies my life is all about being abused and that, Chuck, is not right. Labels like that suck."

As you can see from the cover, my point was well taken.

Okay, it's time to write. Just like my first book, I have no outline. I'm just going to start writing and see what flows. To make sure all cards are on the table, I give fair warning that the following pages will be sprinkled with occasional profanities. If this book aims to reflect the world of kids who have had hard lives, then it should use their language.

For those of you who read my first literary achievement, thanks for returning: It's good to see you again, pal.

1. Appreciating Resistance

Did you ever see the movie *The Perfect Storm*? It's about a crew of deep-sea fishermen, led by George Clooney, who never make it back from their last excursion. The poor suckers get caught in a hurricane. The fierce wind, the awesome waves, and the frigid cold brutalized these men to the point of submission. The sea won; they lost.

Repeated abuse and neglect is my perfect storm. You feel it from the inside out. It can squash your soul like a mammoth wave coming down on a rowboat. Some of us who have been lost at sea swim to shore. Some of us stay adrift and never touch land.

I think I accepted the challenge to write about my life and out-of-home placement to be a beacon; a flashing light that can guide kids, and the adults who care for them, to a safe and happier place. I'm just starting to see land. It's been one ball-buster of a journey.

A couple of days ago, Sally Joshi, the program director at Highland Hills, asked to speak with me. I'm thinking I did something wrong. Turns out, there's a new kid at the program, got here six weeks ago, little guy named Jay, 11, who's caught in his own personal storm.

Sally couldn't tell me much about his history – that confidentiality thing. But she told me that the kid is really hurting. He's fighting being here and won't let anybody get close to him. "His first day was intense." *Been there, done that,* I thought. "He likes his primary counselor,* Paul, but even Paul can't do too much with him," Sally told me.

5

She asked if I would spend some time with him. Help him get adjusted. Maybe get involved for a month or two. "Whoa! Do I look like a therapist?" I shot back.

"No, you're prettier than most therapists," she quipped.

"Aw, shucks, I think I'm gonna blush."

"But you've done some good work here and you know where this kid is coming from. We just want you to help him understand what this place is about – what it does for kids – what it did for you. That's all. Don't go playing shrink."

"Since when do you ask older kids to help younger ones?"

"It's an idea we've been toying with for a while. You're our guinea pig. Are you game?"

"Give me a little lettuce and tell me where I can find this dude."

*Child care workers are often assigned to be primary counselor for one or two kids. A primary might do clothes shopping with the kid, work on goals together, meet once a week, etc. – it's a good thing, a system most programs should use. It's guaranteed attention to kids who need it.

Sebastian Junger wrote *The Perfect Storm* and I don't know who wrote the screenplay. What I do know is that neither writer was on that boat as it was engulfed by the sea's fury. What do men say when the end of life can be measured in moments? Each writer used his imagination to guess the final words of the crew.

I'm going to use my imagination to do the same thing. On the next page, I've recreated part of Jay's first day at the program. I think you should hear about it. I think Jay's life in residential care coupled with my mentoring might provide some good material for this book.

After talking with Sally, I wanted to know more about the kid, so I did a little extracurricular exploring. In other words, I paid Frankie Tavares, a unit mate of Jays, two bucks to *borrow* Jay's log for an hour. (There are a lot of new staff members on his unit; it wasn't a difficult task.) I was particularly curious about that first day:

Why did he come? What were the circumstances? What was going on inside his head? What happened?

As it turns out, the dude reminded me a lot of myself when I first entered residential care.

Jay Comes to Highland Hills

Jay was brought in around 2 p.m. It was a messy transition. He got ripped from his foster home without a chance to say goodbye. One day his acting out scared his foster parents and they called the cops to remove him. He wasn't allowed to go back. He was bullshit.

Around 3 p.m., Jay threw a fit in the dining room. I don't have all the details, but apparently Paul, the senior counselor, instructed all of the other kids to leave the room while he tried to calm Jay down.

Jay: Get the hell away from me!
Paul: Hey, I'm just trying to talk to you. Let's

Jay: not make this such a big deal.

Jay: I said, get the fuck away from me, you asshole! Can't you hear me?

Paul: So you don't want to talk. That's cool. I'll just sit here and keep quiet.

(30 seconds of silence)

Jay: I wish I was dead.

Paul: Man, you seem pretty down on yourself today.

Jay: Fuck you.

(20 second pause)

Paul: This is one crappy day, ain't it?

Jay: Why am I here? I didn't do anything wrong. They just wanted to get rid of me. The fuckin' jerks.

Paul: Are you talking about the Brickmans, your foster family?"

(The kid looks directly into the counselor's eyes.)

Jay: No, I'm talking about your mother...

(20 second pause)

Paul: Well, that explains it. *(switching to his best Tony Soprano voice)* If you's talkin' about my muddah I can unduhstan' why you's so upset. I didn't know you guys had met.

(The two exchange glances. After an awkward pause, Paul cracks a smile. Jay follows suit.)

Paul: Hey, I'm not trying to turn this into a funny thing. But I thought a little humor might help.

Jay: I don't want to stay here. I've heard about these places. They suck!

Paul: Look, I know this is hard to accept, but this is where you'll be for awhile. We're good with kids. You can take that to the bank.

Jay: I'm not staying.

Paul: Do you play basketball?

Jay: Yeah.

Paul: Do you want to go outside and shoot some hoops?

Jay: You got a court?

Paul: Behind the building.

Jay: Okay, but I ain't staying here.

(Paul takes Jay outside. They shoot hoops for 25 minutes. Paul does a lot of trash talking. He tells Jay that he's never lost a one-on-one contest and has a better jump shot than Michael Jordan. Not surprisingly, Paul wins the first game – rubs it in Jay's face a little – and then loses two close games. That's what the good counselors do. Afterwards, the two get a drink at the fountain and then sit and talk under the large Maple tree next to the court.)

Paul: You've got a great jump shot. And who the heck taught you to dribble so well with

	your left hand?
Jay:	I'm a lefty.
Paul:	Yeah, I knew that.
Jay:	Can kids play basketball anytime they want, here?
Paul:	Only the ones I beat.
Jay:	Do you always joke with kids?
Paul:	Do you always play B-ball so well?
Jay:	Yeah.
Paul:	Yeah. So what happened with the Brickmans?
Jay:	They kicked me out of their home for doing nothing wrong.
Paul:	No wonder you're so mad.
Jay:	I was there eight months.
Paul:	That's a long time.
Jay:	They said I touched a neighbor's kid in his private area.
Paul:	Wow. That's a serious thing. If you did that it would have been a big mistake, right?
Jay:	...well...yeah...if I did it. *But I didn't do it.* He probably made it up to screw me. I hate that little bitch, Zack. He's a liar.
Paul:	Does he often make up stories?

(pause)

Jay:	I don't know.
Paul:	Seems like some big mistakes were made, probably by some good people. And now you've got to deal with what happened.
Jay:	I *don't* want to stay here.

Paul: Many kids feel the way you do when they first get here. Hey, on my first day I wanted to quit. A kid threw a chair at me.

Jay: Why did he do that?

Paul: Because I was taking the place of a counselor he really liked. Sometimes kids get angry and misbehave when they have to say good-bye to someone they care about.

(Jay puts his head down and looks as if he's about to cry; but he holds back the tears. They sit together in silence for a few minutes.)

Jay: I.....I...I still don't want to stay here.

Paul: I understand. But why don't you come with me. We'll get you settled. Give it one day. Tomorrow you can call your worker to complain if it's not going well. C'mon.

Jay: Will you be here tomorrow?

Paul: Yeah.

(Jay rises and walks slowly with Paul back to the unit.)

The kid didn't even honeymoon. Came in fighting and hasn't lowered his guard one iota (what the hell is an iota?). From what I understand, he's driving the staff bonkers, hasn't earned any privileges, and wears his anger like a badge. There's got to be a lot of crap festering under his surface. I guess it's time for me to meet him. I'm a little nervous.

Location: Basketball Court

(Paul and Jay are on the court shooting hoops. I approach. "God help me. Don't let me fuck him up even more!")

Paul: This is the older boy I was telling you about, Gus Studelmeyer.

(Jay casts a quick glance at me and continues to shoot baskets.)

Gus: *(in a slightly elevated tone)* Actually, it's Gus "E." Studelmeyer. The E stands for Elvis.

Paul: Excuse me Oh Great One. Jay, this is Gus E. Studelmeyer.

(Jay continues to shoot, ignoring the conversation. This fact is not lost on me.)

Paul: I'm going to leave you guys. I'll be back in a half-hour.

(Paul exits. I watch as Jay continues to dribble and shoot, dribble and shoot...dribble and shoot. He totally ignores me. I don't move or speak. Jay continues to dribble and shoot, dribble and shoot, yes...dribble and shoot. I don't move or speak. From time to time, he glances in my direction but steadfastly avoids eye contact. Twenty-eight minutes later, Paul appears.)

Paul:	How's it going?
Gus:	Great!
Paul:	So you guys had a pretty good first meeting?
Gus:	Absolutely. Can't wait to do it again.

(Jay seems a bit surprised and perhaps unsettled by my positive comments.)

| Paul: | C'mon, Jay. Let's get back to the unit. |

(As he's leaving, I gently grab Jay's arm.)

Gus:	What does my middle name start with?
Jay:	E.
Gus:	What does the E stand for?
Jay:	Elvis.
Gus:	See you soon.
Jay:	Yeah.

Reflections From Our First Encounter

The kid didn't want to talk to me. I can hang with that. I hate when some shirt tries to force stuff out of me. Jay, he's protecting Jay. All he's got is himself. Opening up is risky. Once you let people in, you lose some of yourself. You become part of someone else's story. You expose your weak side. You risk more pain. Shit, it took me a long time before I let some of the inside out.

I know it pisses off (some) staff when troubled kids don't share their feelings, connect with them, or improve their behavior in a significant way. I think a lot of staff members take it personally when they can't get through to one of us.

All I can say to that is, '*Hello, who do you think you're working with? Get over it. Whose needs are you trying to meet, here?*'

I think most kids like me, like Jay, *want* to share our feelings, connect with a significant adult, and improve our behavior; and, I think most of us are trying, but we're just not moving as fast as the folks working with us would like. I think the typical kid in residential care has a different time line than the adults when it comes to making progress. If any staff member could experience first hand what we've experienced, they would understand why.

Hey, I got fucked right up my goddamn ass at least a dozen times. I had a foster parent lock me in a closet for eight hours. My friend, Carlos, was forced to eat vomit by his mother. How soon do you think we should get with the program; in other words, open up to adults and start behaving? Whad'ya think? Three months? Six? Two years? Once you've been taught *not* to trust adults, it becomes a hard lesson to unlearn.

I know it must feel great to the staff when we improve our behavior and start connecting with them, *I just wish they'd feel great about putting in the effort.* Take it from me, Gus E. Studelmeyer, we *really do appreciate* the staff who hang in there with us even when it looks like we're doing shit for work.

Listen to me: Every interaction a staff member has with a hurtin' kid is capable of building trust, of making a difference. From saying hello to us with a smile (after we made your life miserable at bedtime last night), to making sure we get a snack on time.

Ten years from now, I'm not going to remember any great talk I ever had with an adult at Highland Hills. What I will remember is the handful of staff members who stayed the course with me; who treated me with respect, who made me feel good about myself, despite all my gallant attempts to push them away. (Remember Frank, whom I kicked in the balls?)

I'm getting ready to leave Highland Hills. I'm doing better. I believe in myself now. In my head, in my soul, are the folks from this place who got me to this level. I understand that now.

My new friend Jay is a fighter. A commando. A warrior. He communicated with me today. His silence, the ignoring, his desire to put the ball through the hoop, all of these things let me know that he cares about number one, and that he's good – real good – at protecting himself. I might let him know that next time.

He's also terribly alone. I bet some of his acting out is a distraction to avoid sitting with himself. The price we pay for building strong defenses is estrangement.

Wow. Seeing that kid definitely triggered some deep stuff in me.

2. The Times They Are a Changin'

Three days later. Second meeting with Jay. Location: Basketball court.

(Jay is shooting baskets with Paul as I arrive.)

Gus: Hi Paul. Hi Jay.
Paul: How's it going Gus?
Gus: I'm getting by.
Paul: Glad to hear it.

(Paul throws me the basketball)

Gus: Nice pass.
Paul: I'll see you in a half-hour. Don't beat him up too much, Jay.

(Paul leaves. I quickly pass the ball to Jay. He begins dribbling and shooting, dribbling and shooting...dribbling and shooting. I don't move or speak. He's ignoring me again. After 18 minutes, he slows his dribble and then stops altogether, turns, and looks at me.)

Jay: Why did you grab my arm? Isn't that inappropriate PC (personal contact)?
Gus: I guess it could be. I was just trying to get your attention.
Jay: Why are they so fuckin' uptight here about personal contact?
Gus: They're trying to cover their asses and

	keep kids safe.
Jay:	Whad'ya mean?
Gus:	If they don't allow the staff members to touch the kids, and don't allow kids to touch other kids, then no one get touched inappropriately, no one gets sued and the kids are safer. Unfortunately, there's been a lot of bad touchin' going on in places like this. My therapist, Ellen, told me about it.
Jay:	I don't care what you say. I think it's a fucked up thing. It makes you feel like a pervert, like you got a disease.

(Mimicking a staff member)
"Jay, be careful, that was PC."

These assholes don't trust any of us, do they?

Gus:	Some do, some don't. Trust is something you win and then lose. Win/lose. Win/lose. The longer you've got it, the harder it is to lose.
Jay:	So you think the PC rules are good?
Gus:	No, I hate them. When I first got here I felt real angry and unlovable. Pretty much like dirt. I couldn't admit it then, but I liked – needed – getting hugs from the staff, an occasional backrub, an arm around my shoulder, or being tickled. I got to believe it's harder for new kids like you not to get that kind of stuff.
Jay:	Bullshit. I don't need hugs.

Gus:	You don't need hugs right now?
Jay:	No.
Gus:	Right now, you might need some other things.
Jay:	I'm fine.
Gus:	You certainly are good at taking care of yourself.
Jay:	Huh?
Gus:	I think it's *great* the way you protect yourself by pushing people away. It's a real skill. You've got serious talent, dude. Rudeness, defiance, being obnoxious...all of those things make people want to stay away. Hey, they worked for me, too. I did the same shit when I first came. Keep people away and they can't hurt you.
	Unfortunately, you're only eleven. Taking care of yourself – by yourself – is a hard job for someone so young. It's hard for anybody. Plus, if you keep pushing people away, they never get to know what a super kid you are, and you never learn that some folks can be trusted and can help.
	Look man, I'm just telling you what was told to me. I'm no therapist. I don't even know whether you're ready to hear this. I don't want to screw with your brain.
Jay:	I gotta go. There's Paul.
Gus:	Take it easy.

Reflections From Our Second Encounter

Shit, I said too much. Came on too strong. I got to be careful. Seeing where he's at brings me back to my first few months here.

I was ready to watch him play another 30 minutes without any talk. Glad he finally showed some interest. Sad topic he introduced. I'll write about that later. But first, I need to switch gears for a while...

Neil, the activities director, and one of my favorite people of all time, played a stock market game with us last month. He explained buying and selling stocks and taught us a little economics theory. He said, "The only guarantee you have is that stocks go up and then go down. When they go down, and stay down for a while, people start cursing and don't believe the stock market is a good thing. They look elsewhere to put their money. Big mistake. The smart people, the ones who know about up and down cycles, keep investing *wisely* and usually end up in a good place."

It's the same thing with residential treatment, which is probably down right now. But folks shouldn't give up on it. Because it's still a great place for a really hurting kid and his family who need the safety, security, and therapeutic help this form of care provides. In time, I believe the problem areas will dissipate and the field will be up again.

Why do I think RT is struggling? Hey, take a look around. At Highland Hills we never have enough staff members. And some of the ones they do hire simply aren't cut out for this kind of work. Consequently, we have a lot more problems. Pick an area: Physical restraint, *touching*, bedtimes, meals, activities, transition times – there are problems with each one. And talk about throwing fuel on a fire: the kids they're bringing in nowadays seem a lot more troubled. Sadly, a higher percentage appears to be struggling with psychiatric- and neurological-type conditions.

We now have kids living here who have personality disorders, eating disorders, bi-polar, ODD, ADD, ADHD, OCD, PTSD, CD, PDD (you get the sense that the letter "D" is not a good letter?) I feel for them. But I know they can be helped here.

Some of the kids are told their diagnoses and use this information as a crutch. Elmore is always yelling "I'm ODD...I'm ODD, don't make me do this." I understand that some staff complain about the kids being told. I've never asked. Elmore approached me recently:

"Hey, Gus, I'm ODD, ADHD, and CD. What are you?"

"AOL," I told him.

"Shit, never heard that one, Gus. You must really be fucked up."

I've heard through the grapevine that residential centers everywhere are hurting for staff and taking in tougher kids. Doesn't seem like a good combination, does it?

What a set-up! You hire people without the proper experience and skills to work in an undermanned environment with increasingly difficult kids and then get mad at them when a screw-up occurs. It's silly and sad. So what gives?

Look, I don't want to spend too much time talking about what's currently wrong with residential care, that's not why I agreed to write this book. But it would be crazy for me not to address the issue. Besides, I'm just a kid. I don't have all the information or the answers.

A few hours ago I visited Dr. Pittsiotti in his office. He's the executive director. I figured he'd have some good insights. Needless to say, he didn't want to talk turkey, so I hypnotized him. It wasn't hard.

"You're getting sleepy, sleepy...your eyelids are getting heavier..."

The guy talked my ear off. He's not a happy camper. He's worried about the field. Like I said, I don't want to dwell on this. Here's an excerpt from our conversation that pretty much sums up the good, bad, and ugly of residential treatment as we know it today:

Dr. P: You want answers, Gus? Okay listen carefully: States and towns pay for kids to live in residential centers. And it costs a lot of money to stay in one of these places. Most states and towns don't like having to pay a lot of money - we're talkin' millions of dollars every year. So, they don't always give us enough money to do the job right, and lack of funding causes huge problems for programs and kids like you.

One of the main reasons you're seeing some really hurtin' kids come through the doors is because the states have no choice but to place them in residential centers – and we have no choice but to accept them; these kids couldn't possibly function in less restrictive settings (i.e. less costly). But the kind of kid we accepted a few years ago, the angry, confused, victim of abuse – a kid like you, Gus – well, that kid often ends up in foster care now, even though some of them clearly need the structure, security and treatment of a group care setting. Like I said, much of this is because of the Benjamins.

Gus: Who the hell are the Benjamins? Why are they such jerks?

Dr. P: The Benjamins is a slang term for money. Get it? Benjamins, as in Ben Franklin's face on a bill.

Gus: Oh yeah, I knew that.

Dr. P: Gus, if we could pay our child care workers five-thousand dollars more per year, provide more training, and improve the staff-to-child ratios at most centers, many of the problems in our field would go away. I really believe that. But the states don't want to pay.

Gus: The bastards! Don't they have any feelings?

Dr. P: Whoa...Gus. Don't be so quick to blame the states. Some of them are reluctant to give us more money because: they have intense budgetary constraints and we

	simply haven't proven that we're worth it.
Gus:	Whaddaya talkin' about? This place has helped hundreds of kids, including me. Ain't that proof enough?
Dr. P:	It's not that simple. The people who research this stuff haven't determined that troubled kids leaving residential care do any better than troubled kids who got some alternative form of help. So, some states question whether our huge price tag and entire form of treatment is worth it.
Gus:	Are you kidding me? I can't believe that a kid who gets good residential care doesn't do better than the same kind of kid who gets less.
Dr. P:	That's the fact, Jack.
Gus:	Do you think that makes sense? And remember, you're still under hypnosis. That means no B.S.
Dr. P:	Of course not. I think residential care, and by this I mean any form of out-of-home treatment, is still a truly effective modality. Even with all the changes that have occurred, I still believe we're helping. I wouldn't be here if I thought otherwise.
Gus:	So why don't kids leaving residential settings do better?
Dr. P:	Because many of the kids being discharged end up in situations where they and their caretakers don't get enough support. Think about it: The first day a

kid wakes up after leaving a residential setting, she usually doesn't have as many friends around; doesn't have the same therapist; doesn't have an activity department ready to do things with her; doesn't have a group of adults ready to help her and her family if there is a crisis; and she is often unfamiliar with the environment and misses the safety and security of group care. Get the point? When a kid leaves a residential setting, the lack of support leaves her and her family (or caretakers) incredibly vulnerable.

It's often at this very point that kids and families need us the most.

Some folks think residential care should help a kid to ascend to a new level of functioning that is internalized and permanent. What a crock! *Residential care doesn't fix kids.* Not enough people get this point. A good residential setting boosts a kid's self esteem, helps him, and hopefully his family, work through important psychological stuff, and gives them all new skills and ways of thinking to function better in the world. But if a troubled kid leaves residential treatment and goes to an environment where the overall level of care is dramatically diminished, then the odds are good for her to have trouble adjusting.

This issue drives me nuts. A state might pay close to $100,000 a year for a kid to live at a residential treatment center, yet the day after she's discharged the kid wakes up in a home or foster care setting that is appreciably less funded, in other words, has radically fewer services and support. It's no big mystery why some kids return to group care settings after they're discharged.

If I were the Czar of Child Welfare, I wouldn't allow a kid to enter a residential facility unless that facility made a commitment to stay with the kid and his family for *years* after he was discharged. In the business, it's called "aftercare." Not enough programs do it adequately...because few are paid to do it at all.

Imagine if every kid who left home for college was told that she could no longer have contact with her family.

"You're in college now. You've ascended to a new level of functioning. You don't need your family anymore. Don't touch that phone!"

Although I exaggerate, what the typical kid experiences when she leaves a residential setting isn't very different.

Gus: I think I get what you're saying. But you do have me a tad confused. Earlier you said, "Gus, if we could pay our child care workers another five-thousand dollars per year, provide more training, and improve the staff-to-child ratios at most centers, many of the problems in our field would go away."

Dr. P: How the hell can you recite that word for word?

Gus: I'm a genius, remember?

Well, anyway, you made that statement, but you also said that residential care (RC) is a "truly effective" form of treatment.

Doc, how can it be so effective if there are so many problems?

In addition, you said that if a kid goes from RC to an environment where there isn't enough support, he has a high probability of floundering. So what's the deal? Even if the problems in residential care were fixed by giving every youth worker a five-thousand dollar salary increase, won't the aftercare issue still be there? Seems to me like you're contradicting yourself, big guy.

Dr. P: Gus, You are one sharp dude.

Gus: Stop kissing my hiney and answer the questions.

Dr. P: Okay.

First of all let's define what the term *success* means as it applies to residential care. To me, we're successful if we get into a kid's head and get him to believe in himself; if we boost his self-esteem, teach him some self-management skills, and have him leave knowing that there are people – like us – in the world *who think he's special.*

It's been said, and I think proven through research, that one caring adult can make a huge difference in child's life and his future. I'd like to believe that many kids who enter group care meet at least one (and usually more) caring adults along the way.

I periodically get calls from kids that I worked with years ago. Many of them are doing okay. Each one of them wants to know about the staff members who worked with them.

"Hey, Pittsiotti, do you ever hear from Jill Hokpins? She was cool. I remember she always had a great snack waiting for us after school. She also was the one I turned to when I was taken away from my family."

"Doc, this is Billy Frost. How ya doin' man? Still playing one-on-one with the kids? Remember the time I shot the ball over the backboard and it hit your wife on the head? Is the lump gone?"

"Pitts, is Roger still a supervisor? He used to take all of us fishin'. Those were some of the best days of my life. I take my kid fishin', a lot."

I can tell in their voices how much we meant to them; how much we're *still* with them. In fact, some of our former residents continue to call our staff members on a weekly basis. I never discourage it, because in some cases, we're the only folks who ever gave a damn about 'em. They need us.

We all go through life being guided by people who get in our heads, people who believe in us. We never forget that here.

Sure, we do a lot of other good things to help kids, like teach them how to self-manage their behavior and learn important life skills, provide individual, group, and family therapy...yada, yada, yada.

But, man, I still think our most important work is about making a connection with a kid...formin' that ol' relationship.

Gus: *I get it, Doc.* But you still haven't answered the question. What good is residential care if kids screw up when they leave – even if they do establish some *awesome* relationships?

Dr. P: The answer, which I've tried to explain, is that the success of residential care shouldn't be judged primarily by how a kid does right after being discharged. I think it's great that the field is becoming more conscious about outcomes and accountability, but on the other hand I heard a guy from New York say, "You can't quantify the human soul." *Success* is a relative term.

I think the value of a good residential stay might not show up until a kid is older, perhaps even an adult. Like I said earlier, it almost doesn't matter how well we do with a kid if he goes to an environment where there isn't enough support for him and his caretakers – and this happens far too often. And when it does, people blame us for not preparing the kid properly, and question our effectiveness. *And that really pisses me off!* Because that kid *is* better. And he'll *do* better if and when the environment provides enough support. If appropriate support never comes, he'll probably have trouble, but later in life, when some maturity kicks in and his brain is fully developed, his time in residential care will pay nice dividends.

Should there be better aftercare practices in place? You bet, but good residential care makes a difference.

Gus: Man, you sound like you're running for office.

Dr. P: In some respects I am. Our field is currently under a huge microscope. People are questioning everything we do. Folks like me have to get the message out – almost like a politician – or the powers that be will keep changing these places until they're no longer effective. They'll keep focusing on the symptoms and neglect the problems.

Wow. That man can talk. I'm sure glad he's on our side. I hope people listen.

The stock market thing and my talk with Pittsiotti were included to provide some context for the issues being kicked around in this book. It doesn't make sense to talk about symptoms (i.e. more and more rules and conservative approaches) without exploring the underlying problems.

Back to my friend...

Jay is ticked off about the PC thing. I don't blame him. All kids need physical affection. Once it starts getting outlawed the ramifications are terrible. We shouldn't have to worry so much about touching others. Sure, some of us who have problems in this area need firm rules around what is appropriate touching and what isn't – but sometimes we're made to feel like lepers.

Juanita works on my unit. She's a very warm and caring person. She's probably in the touchy-feely camp. In the old days, I'm sure she'd be hugging and grabbing us kids (appropriately, of course) till we couldn't breathe. We'd have loved it. Although few would admit it.

Nowadays, Juanita has to follow the rules. She can't go around hugging teenagers. Last Thursday was a rough day for me. As I was walking home from school, I got teased by a group of thugs. They were calling me fat and making fun of my clothes. One of them rode me hard for living at the Hills. "Are you a retard, Gussy boy? Is that why you live in the looney bin?" "I hear you're all queers. Are you a fag, Gussy

31

boy?" "Do you want to suck mine, Gussy boy?"

I got back to the unit and just flung my book bag across the room. Juanita tried to talk to me and I told her to fuck off. I then stormed to my room, closed the door and began to cry. A few minutes later Juanita appeared. She sat in my doorway for five minutes. She's not allowed to come in. That's a new rule. No staff member can be alone with a kid in a confined space.

After I stopped crying, I told her about being teased. Man, it really affected her. Her eyes welled up with tears and then she did something pretty damn cool.

"Gus, I'd like to give you a big hug right now. But I can't. But I would like you to step into the hallway, please."

I walked into the hallway.

"Shake my hand and listen."

I shook her hand and listened.

"From now on, every time I give you a handshake I want you to imagine it's a hug. Got it?"

"Got it," I said.

She started to walk away.

"Wait!" I yelled.

I ran up to her and stuck out my hand.

I'm sure Juanita would rather work in a place where physical affection isn't taboo. But she chooses to stay here. Instead of complaining and breaking the rules because she doesn't agree with them, she does the best she can with the cards she is dealt. I wish there were more Juanitas. I think many staff members are fed up with these kind of changes. They're fed up with residential settings becoming so cold and sterile, and they either walk around with an angry attitude, or quit.

I guess the new, more conservative rules around touching came about because of kids being touched improperly by staff members in places like the Hills. But if you believe what the Doc had to say, these new rules wouldn't be necessary if places like the hills could hire more qualified people and train them better.

Ten years from now I'm going to come back to the Hills for a visit. I hope to see staff members hugging kids and making them laugh. And during those ten years I'll be working hard to make sure that happens.

We can shake on that promise.

3. Holding and Scolding

Physical restraint has become a BIG DEAL at Highland Hills. My sources tell me it's become a BIG DEAL throughout the country. When I first entered the program, kids could be taken to the floor for a host of reasons. Some staff members were quick on the trigger; they'd grab you for blowing your friggin' nose wrong. Not any more. Now, they're only supposed to hold you if you're hurting yourself or others.

A whole new set of guidelines has been instituted. Most of them make sense, but some seem difficult for staff to meet, and there is still a lot of discretion factored in to the equation. I guess I like the changes and the attention they're giving to this, but there's still a lot of ironing that needs to get done, if you catch my drift.

I was supposed to have my third meeting with Jay today. But the kid got restrained instead. Damn. From what I can gather, it wasn't a pretty scene. Here's what went down:

Nomar Flood, Jay's roommate, returned from a home visit around 3:30 p.m. He was in excellent spirits. His visit went well. He paraded into the kitchen brandishing pictures of his family. One of the photos was of his paternal grandfather, Ike, whom he had never met. His dad found it while doing some cleaning in their apartment.

Jim Parcel was the childcare worker on duty when Nomar entered. There were only a few kids on the unit; most had gone out on an activity. Jay was with his therapist, Dan.

Nomar (His real name is Norman, but ever since Nomar Garciappara, all-star shortstop for the Boston Red Sox, won the AL batting title, he's insisted on being called Nomar. His parents approved. Frankly, methinks Nomar sounds a lot cooler than Norman.)

Nomar excitedly shows Jim the pictures. He rarely gets so animated. Jim is impressed. "Look at my grand dad. My father said he was over six feet tall. He worked for a big railroad company for over thirty years. Went all over the country."

Jim patiently sat with Nomar as he described each picture in great detail. I've met Jim. He's okay in my book. (And this *is* my book.)

Around 4:15 p.m., Lynell, the head of activities, dropped in and scooped up all the kids. Someone had just donated Red Sox tickets and she was going to take them. As soon as Nomar heard RED SOX, he dropped the pictures, grabbed his glove and flew to her van. Nomar doesn't get too excited about much; the Red Sox are an exception. He's had a tenuous relationship with his father. His mother died of AIDS when he was four.

I think pictures are a big deal for a kid like Nomar, a kid like me. When your past has been shaky, a picture becomes a solid reminder that you come from somewhere; that you're part of family; that you have some positive history squeezed in with all the negative crappola.

Lynell takes all of the kids in the house. Jim is alone. A few minutes later, Jerry Edwards strolls through the door. He's a relatively new childcare worker, been at the Hills for five months; a little rough around the edges but he has a good heart and truly likes kids. Jerry goes to the staff room and reads the logs. Returns to the kitchen, stokes up some coffee, and asks Jim about the day.

After filling Jerry in, Jim gets up and heads to the staff room. He takes four or five logs that he's been writing in with him. He's off in ten minutes. It's been a long shift. He can almost smell that Big Mac simmering on the grill. Jim's from the Midwest; eats meat like he never heard of cholesterol. As he exits the kitchen, he turns back and asks Jerry a favor:

"Oh, Jerry, Nomar returned with some pictures of his grandfather. They mean a lot to him. Could you please put them in his cubby? Thanks."

Jerry nods. Nomar's personal, locked cubby is in a closet right off the kitchen. Jerry sees the pictures but chooses to finish his coffee, read an old sports page, and do a little doodling (he has a talent for drawing). He'll take care of the pictures later. There's no rush. Hey, it's not often that a child care worker finds himself alone, and has the luxury of sippin', doodlin', and readin'. Two minutes later, the door squeaks open and Jay enters with Dan.

Jay:	Fuck you, asshole. I don't care if I ever see you again.
Dan:	Jay, can we go somewhere and talk about this.
Jay:	Get the hell out of here!
Dan:	I'm not gonna push this. You know the deal.
Jay:	Shut up!

(Jay grabs an apple from a fruit bowl. Angrily sits down at the kitchen table, turns his seat away form Dan, and begins eating it)

Dan: *(addressing Jerry in a calm voice)* We had a difficult session. Some things came up that were hard to deal with. On the way back he tried to trip me.

Jerry: Do you want us to drop his level or give him some kind of consequence?

Dan: Not this time. I want to process this with him and use natural consequences. Next time we meet, we'll stay in my office instead of walking around campus.

Jerry: Okay. I get you.

Dan: He's upset. I think he needs to be close to an adult for a while.

Jerry: We'll do that.

Dan: Thanks. *(addressing Jay)* We had a hard meeting. I know you're feeling pretty bad right now. Hang in there. I'll come by tomorrow.

Jerry: Get lost. You're full of shit.

Dan: Okay, I got to go. Take care, guys.

(Dan exits.)

Jerry: Man, seems like you had a rough one.

Jay: Leave me the fuck alone. I don't want to talk.

Jerry: Hey, I was just trying to help.

(Jay turns his head and ignores Jerry. A few sec-

onds later, he gets up and starts walking around the kitchen. There's a look of malevolence in his eyes. As he passes the activity calendar on the wall, he grabs it with his right arm, rips the top sheet, and shreds it.)

Jay: Guess they'll be no fuckin' activities this month.

(Jerry's anxiety level begins to rise.)

Jerry: Jay, knock it off. You don't need to do that.
Jay: I don't *need* to do any fuckin' thing.

(After annihilating the calendar, Jay calmly continues his stroll through the kitchen. At precisely the same moment, both Jay and Jerry notice Nomar's pictures on the counter.)

("Oh, shit!" Jerry thinks to himself. "Don't do anything to those pictures. I should have put them away. Fuck! I'm really gonna get screwed if he touches them.")

(Jay grabs the pictures and examines them.)

Jay: Who the fuck is this old fart?
Jerry: *(with an accelerated heart beat)* C'mon Jay. Please put the pictures down. They belong to Nomar. It's his grandfather.

(Time seems to stop as Jay ponders what to do.

39

Jerry can't seem to read the expression on Jay's face. He thinks he might have witnessed a tinge of sadness)

Jay: Who cares?

(Jay begins ripping the pictures.)

Jerry: No! Stop it!

(With a spiteful smile, Jay continues to rip away.)

Jerry: *(angrily)* That's really dumb! You *didn't* need to do that. Nomar's going to be really upset.

(At this point, Jim appears with his traveling bag. He was all set to leave.)

Jim: *(addressing Jerry)* What's going on, Jerry?
Jerry: Jim, Jay had a rough meeting with Dan. He's having a hard time settling in. He destroyed the calendar and just ripped up Normar's pictures.
Jim: *(trying his very best to control his emotions)* Why didn't you put them away?
Jerry: I was going to. He just popped in. I didn...didn't have any time.

(Jay ignores the conversation, but does notice a felt-tipped marker that Jerry had been doodling with. Within a second or two, it's in his left hand.)

Jim: *(addressing Jay)* Hey, buddy, why don't

we go outside and talk – maybe shoot some baskets. I want to show a move I taught Shaq last week.

(Jim's attempt to deescalate using distraction and humor doesn't work. Jay walks to the near wall and scribbles, THIS PLACE SUCKS on it.)

Jim: C'mon, man, don't make things worse. Put the pen down and you and I can talk.

(Jay continues to ignore what is being said.)

Jim: Hey, aren't you supposed to see Gus today? He's my main man. You can't see him if you're not in good shape.

(No response from Jay)

Jim: Jerry, please call the supervisor on duty and tell her what's happening.

(Jerry walks to the kitchen phone and calls.)

Jim: Look, I know a lot went down today, but you don't need to pile up a lot of conse-quences and-

Jay: *(calmly)* Fuck you. What do I got to lose, asshole?

(In essence, he was correct. Jay still hadn't earned many privileges and there weren't any meaningful consequences to dangle over him.)

Jerry: Sally said to keep her posted and to remind Jay that he'll be responsible for any damage he commits, and that the police can be called if he seriously damages property.

(Jay walks over to the opposite wall and scribbles: Jerry is a Homo.*)*

Jerry: *(visibly upset)* Hey, knock it off. That's ridiculous! This is getting carried away.

Jim: Jerry, why don't you go in the other room-

(Underneath the word Homo, *Jay writes:* He likes to suck boys dicks.*)*

Jerry: *(with agitation)* This is crazy. He *needs* to stop.

Jim: Jerry, he's not hurting himself or others. We don't hold kids anymore for damaging property. You know that. I know this is hard.

*(*Jerry sucks Jims prick *is scribbled.)*

(Jerry approaches Jay.)

Jim: Jerry, why don't you go-

Jerry: *(staring...glaring down at Jay)* Give me the pen right now.

Jim: Jerry-

(Jay keeps writing. Jerry puts his hand on Jay's forearm. His hope is to escort him to another room. In response to Jerry's touch, Jay whips his arm around and smacks Jerry right across the face. Jerry is stunned. Jim instantly moves to restrain Jay with Jerry's beleaguered help. Jay resists mightily.)

Jay: Get the fuck off of me! Get off me! Let me go! You're hurting me! You can't do this! I wasn't hurting anybody!

(Using new restraint techniques, Jim and Jerry maneuver Jay into a sitting-type position. Jim is behind Jay holding his arms while Jerry controls his legs.)

Jim: *(calmly)* Relax, Jay. You're okay.

(Jay tries to head-butt Jim in his face, and barely misses.)

Jim: You're okay.

Jay: Let me go! You didn't need to hold me! LET ME GO!

(Jim and Jerry remain quiet.)

Jay: You're humpin' me. I can feel it. You're humpin' me. Get the FUCK OFF! GET THE FUCK OFF....Get off....GET OFF. I'm gonna get you guys fired.

(Jim and Jerry remain quiet)

Jay: Get the FUCK OFF! You're all assholes! Ow! Don't hold me so tight. You're hurting me.

Jim: Try and take some deep breaths, it might-

Jay: *(quieter)* Fuckin' bitches!

(Jim and Jerry remain quiet.)

(Fifteen minutes into the restraint Jay wears down, and tears form in his eyes. He wants to cry but once again holds back. The fight is gone. Jerry and Jim hold Jay for another four or five minutes, progressively loosening their grips. He eventually is able to walk with Jim to the quiet room and process the episode. As usual, he didn't say much. He's not ready to trust.)

The next day Jerry got in big trouble. How do I know? The sucker got suspended pending a review. Witnesses report that he looked quite upset after meeting with Sally, the Program Director. It's not hard to guess what transpired during their meeting. After empathizing with the guy, I'm sure it went along these lines:

Sally: Why did you put your arm on him?

Jerry: Because he was losing control and appeared to be a safety risk to himself and others.

Sally: I guess I'm a little confused. Jim wrote in the incident report that Jay calmly scribbled the sexual comments on the wall. Was he mistaken?

Jerry: You know what he wrote. It was disgusting.

Sally: Yeah. It was pretty graphic. As I said before, it must have been awful to stand there and feel so helpless.

Jerry: Yeah. It sucked. I couldn't believe we were letting him get away with it.

Sally: So, he probably was calm as he wrote?

Jerry: Look, he may have appeared calm, but you could sense it building in him. He was like a time-bomb ready to blow. He would have kept pushin' and pushin' until someone got hurt. You can tell.

Sally: Hey, you might be right. But that's not how we do it anymore.

Jerry: Bullshit! We can use our discretion if we feel safety is being threatened. I should have intervened when he picked up Nomar's pictures. Nomar had a fit when he learned what Jay did. The whole unit is a lot more tense now.

Sally: These aren't easy calls. But here's the bottom line: safety *was* not being threatened.

Jerry: That's *your* bottom line. *Your* interpretation. *You* weren't there. This is bogus! We never let kids get away with this shit before. This ain't right.

Sally: Do you really think so?

Jerry: Yes. Forget what this did to Nomar, the kid could have caused hundreds of dollars of damage.

Sally: So?

Jerry: So? So! That's not okay.

Sally: In most cases like this, we deescalate the kid without physical intervention. Kids get meaningful consequences, we thoroughly process the incident, and we find the money to promptly repair the damage. In some cases, we might call the police. If a kid repeatedly destroys property we'll put him on a special contract and/or incentive program; if he keeps it up we might even terminate him from the program.

Jerry: You know how cops deal with our kids. It's much better if we take care of them. And how does terminating a troubled kid help him? They come here angry and resistant. Many lack the internal controls to manage themselves well. You tell us their acting out is a message. What kind of response is terminating a kid who is telling us, through his extreme behavior, that he needs *our* kind of help? That's nuts.

Sally: You're right about some of this. And sometimes folks like me have to have tough talks with folks like you around discretionary decisions. Believe me, this ain't much fun for me, either.

But you've got to look at the big picture. Kids have *died* being held, countless others, including staff, have been injured.

46

The new guidelines, although not perfect, have the right intentions. We were just too loose about this for too long a time – and kids and staff paid the price.

Look, I know the changes around physical intervention are hard to deal with, but – for the most part – they really do make sense. Restraints are at times necessary, but it's too intense an intervention to be done unless it's absolutely warranted, processed, and documented.

Jerry: So what happens next?

Sally: We have to suspend you indefinitely until the incident has been reviewed by the Division for Children and Families

Jerry: Are you kidding me?

Sally: It's become standard procedure.

Jerry: That's just unbelievable.

Sally: Hey, it's not great for us, either. It's not like we have tons of people ready to fill your slot. Every time this happens it handcuffs the program and negatively affects the kids.

Jerry: I feel like telling you guys to stuff this friggin' job. Who needs this kind of shit? I still don't think I did anything wrong and I bet a lot of people would agree with me.

Sally: I don't blame you for feeling the way you do. It's never been harder to work here and that's why it's never been more important. Don't make any rash decisions. I'll call you on Monday.

Jerry: *(Jerry puts his head down and grows somber)* You know, I may not be the best childcare worker in this place. I may never be able to talk with kids like Jim Parcel does. But I like being here and I thought I was doing okay. For the first time in my life I had a job that made me feel good about myself. Maybe I was wrong. Maybe I'm not cut out for this. Maybe it just ain't worth it anymore.

Sally: It is worth it, and you do make a difference here. We all feel like crap when something like this happens. This has happened to me, as well.

Remember what we say here. Self-esteem injuries occur all the time in residential care. Fifteen times a day something happens that makes you feel like shit and we take it personally. A kid won't do what you ask, a group is out of control, a supervisor criticizes you, a good talk does nothing. But they're all injuries that heal. Like a cut on your finger, they will pass with time.

Today you suffered a serious emotional injury. It will take some time, but it should heal. Make a good decision, man. You're important to us.

Jerry: I'll talk to you on Monday. I'm not sure I'm going to stay here. You're right about one thing. I am taking this personally and I don't know if I can handle any more injuries. This sucks.

Change is a bitch. I've been hearing that for years. I guess it's true. This restraint stuff is complicated. When I first heard about the changes, I struggled with them. On the surface, it doesn't seem right that one of us should be allowed to physically trash a program without staff members trying to intervene; but, on the other hand, the rule probably reduces the amount of restraints that occur – which ain't a bad thing. Damage can be repaired. Physical and emotional trauma are harder to fix.

I was blown away when I heard that kids have actually died while being held. God, what a terrible thing. I hurt for the kids who died and their families; I hurt for the staff members who were involved.

Kids like me come to residential treatment angry and resistant. We do all that we can to take care of number one. With help, we get our act together and begin to realize that other people have feelings. I have learned over the years to actually consider how my behavior makes a staff member feel.

Frankly, I think that's a good way to judge if a kid has made progress in one of these places: Does he think about other people's feelings and situations? I never did before, but I now appreciate the sacrifices many childcare counselors make to work in places like this. The hours suck, the pay stinks, and we dudes don't always treat them with much respect. Sure, some jerks end up working in these places, but I think the good ones outweigh the bad. So, I really do feel for the kids *and* the staff members when I hear about tragic restraints.

I think some of the restraint issues are about power and control. Man, it must be hard to stand back and watch a kid scribble you're a homo on a wall, or call you every name in the book. You got to be one strong dude to handle that well. And don't forget what Pittsiotti said, a lot of the problems in the field are the result of not having enough skilled professionals because of the tough working conditions.

Although the new restraint rules are designed to help kids, they require staff members to be even more adept at this stuff. Hello out there? Is any body listening? You're asking staff to do more even though programs are coping with less. I occasionally hear Sally bitching that's it's impossible to get all the staff in for trainings. You don't have to be a genius (even though I am) to figure out that more sophisticated treatment requires more training. So who loses if they don't get it?

Everyone.

Final thoughts:

This restraint stuff presents some complex issues. Some kids need to be held. I did. I came to this program angry, confused, and I was one impulsive/aggressive son of a gun. My therapist would tell you that I lacked internal controls. (Every time she says this, I envision metal gears and valves crankin' inside of me.) Fortunately, I had some good staff members who knew how to restrain a kid and talk to him afterwards. They helped me work through some of my junk and learn more self-control.

But if restraint isn't done right, the results can be

disastrous. So I'm glad it's getting all this attention. I just hope people don't go too far. Troubled kids need to feel safe. If we see kids destroying property and acting in ways that scare us – and no one does anything about it – well, that ain't good, either. (Heck, if we're the ones doing that stuff and no one tries to stop us – *we* often get scared and feel unsafe; and the experience doesn't help much on the learning self-control front)

It would be nice if physical restraint weren't necessary. But as long as there are kids full of rage who lack the internal controls to self manage, restraint will be a necessary intervention. It's just got to be done right.

4. Hellos and Goodbyes
Part One

Third meeting with Jay. Place: Basketball court

Gus: How's it going man?

Jay: Throw me the ball.

(Jay shoots for a while, ignoring me.)

Gus: You had a rough day last week. I'm sorry we didn't get to meet.

(Jay continues to shoot.)

Gus: Something must have really ticked you off, eh?

(Jay slows his bounce, pondering what I said. Suddenly he turns and whips the basketball at me. I don't react in time and take it square in the gut. It knocks the wind out of me and I double over in agony. I can see Jay's feet. I think he's just staring at me. After a minute or two...normal breathing returns)

Gus: What the hell was that for?

Jay: I felt like it.

Gus: Could you let me know next time you feel like it? I think I almost cracked a rib.

Jay: Are you okay?

Gus: I'll live.

(Jay picks up the ball and turns his back to me. After a long pause...)

Jay: You ever been in foster care?
Gus: Is that what this is all about?
Jay: *(angrily)* Just tell me, asshole!
Gus: Yeah. I was in three of them.

(Jay turns around and faces me.)

Jay: Did you ever hear from any of the foster parents after you left their home?
Gus: I dunno. Let me think ... One of my families, the Foleys, sent me a card on my birthday – but I never saw *any* of them after I left. I got booted from all three 'cause of my behavior. I don't think they wanted any piece of me. It was good riddance to Ol' Gus.
Jay: So none of them liked you anymore?
Gus: I don't know. Maybe they liked me but couldn't handle my behavior.
Jay: I bet they thought you were a bad kid.
Gus: Maybe. But I wasn't an easy kid, then. I had a lot goin' on.

(Gus notices that Jay's eyes have moistened.)

Gus: Were you in foster care?
Jay: *(pause)* The Brickmans kicked me out of their home. They said I touched a neigh-

54

bor's kid in his private area.

Gus: Did you make that mistake?

Jay: No. The kid lied about it.

Gus: That's too bad.

Jay: My therapist, Dan, told me last week that the Brickmans will never let me back into their home. He said they're not sure if they'll even visit me. I haven't heard from them since I got here.

Gus: That really sucks. I liked some of the families that I was with. Do you kind of like the Brickmans?

Jay: They're okay. They might have adopted me.

Gus: Had they mentioned that?

Jay: Yeah.

Gus: Man, that really does suck.

(For the first time since coming to Highland Hills, Jay begins to cry. He sits down on the hardtop and covers his face with his hands. I don't know what to do... what to say. I feel helpless standing next to him. I sit beside the little guy and gently put my arm around his shoulder. My arm sways as he begins to rhythmically rock back and forth. Suddenly, I find myself adrift in a sea of losses. I think about my mother abandoning me for five years; how I cried when Margaret, my favorite counselor left the program. And for some ungodly reason, I think about my dead father, a man I never met. I ache for him. Why the hell did he have to die? Why couldn't I have known him?)

For a moment I am lost within myself. Jay's tears, and my own, bring me back to the present.

Jay: Are you crying?
Gus: Yeah.
Jay: Why?
Gus: I was thinking about the people I've lost in my life.

(Jay doesn't respond verbally. He puts his head down and we sit quietly for five minutes)

Gus: C'mon. Let's shoot a few hoops.

(We shoot around for five to ten minutes and then return to our cottages. We didn't say much to each other. I think we were both feeling lost.)

When I returned to my room, I asked to speak with my therapist, Ellen. Luckily, we caught her as she was about to leave. Naturally, she agreed to stay and talk with me. That's Ellen.

Ellen: What's up? You look awful.
Gus: I had a rough meeting with Jay today.
Ellen: What happened?
Gus: He threw a basketball at me.
Ellen: Did you provoke him?
Gus: *(animated)* No! I didn't do a thing. He just whipped it at me. He's hurting because his foster family kicked him out and don't want him back. They were talking about adopting him.

Ellen:	That would get me to throw a basketball at someone.
Gus:	They accused him of touching a neighbor's kid in his genital area. Jay denies it. Do you think he's lying?
Ellen:	What do you think?
Gus:	Why did I think you'd ask me what I think?
Ellen:	Well?
Gus:	It's obvious the kid has a hard time opening up. He doesn't trust anyone. If he did touch that kid, I doubt he'd admit it.
Ellen:	Sounds like a kid I once knew.
Gus:	Who?
Ellen:	Hello...anyone there?
Gus:	Oh yeah, me.
Ellen:	We couldn't talk about your mother abandoning you for quite a while.
Gus:	It's still hard, even though she's been back in my life for a few years.
Ellen:	Some scars don't go away. You learn to live with them. Maybe see them as a symbol of personal courage.
Gus:	*(Gus lowers his head and remains quiet for 10-20 seconds)*...I cried.
Ellen:	I know. You cried a lot when we started the work. It was hard.
Gus:	NO! I CRIED TODAY...with Jay. I couldn't control myself. I got all choked up and started whimpering like a baby. What a wuss!
Ellen:	His stuff hit home, eh?
Gus:	It was so sad, Ellen. Here's this kid whose

57

been trying so hard to stay cool, stay tough, and he's crumbling before my eyes. I could tell he really loved the Brickmans, his foster parents. Losing them is tearing him up inside. And it's not just the loss; it's how it happened. One day he's a kid expecting to be adopted by a family he cares about. The next day: BANG! He's ripped from their home, and they don't ever want to see him again. How the hell is he ever going to say hello to a new family?

Ellen: I bet there's more here than meets the eye. If Jay had a strong connection with the Brickmans, then they must have had a strong one with him, as well. There must have been some bad stuff going down in that home for them to act this way.

Gus: Look, I know how it goes. Jay probably loved them but had a hard time showing it. When you've been abused and neglected it's not always easy to relate "appropriately" with the ones caring for you. You're always on edge, afraid they're going to hurt and reject you. Why do so many people think acting out means we don't care about the folks looking out for us?

"Listen, boy, if you really want to stay here, you'll improve that behavior of yours."

It's fuckin' ridiculous. Are we just supposed to just ignore reality? Pretend that we can trust folks; understand what a normal relationship is all about? Give up on some necessary testing? And forget about this psychological crap, some of us simply don't know *how* to act in a family or one of these places. We need time to learn the social shit. Sometimes it ain't about the anger, it's about the skills. *The ones we don't got.* God, this pisses me off.

Ellen: Your tears weren't just for Jay?

Gus: *(after a lengthy pause)* No. They were for every stinkin' person I've lost. The fucking Dad I never knew; the three foster families who never contacted me after they booted me out; my mother for leaving me too many times, and all the folks I've met along the way who have come and gone. God, I was there with Jay. I mean, I was *there* with him.

Ellen: Loss sucks.

Gus: Did you say "sucks?"

Ellen: It fit.

Gus: Man, it's so hard to get on with your life when you you've got such heavy crappola behind you. The losses...they haunt us. They're like ghosts lurking in the wind. You try to take a step forward, but you're immediately blown back, grabbed by an unseen force that tauntingly whispers in your ear, *"Where the hell you going, buddy? You've got unfinished business.*

You can't leave."

Ellen: Do you remember the dream sequence from Chapter Three in the first Gus book?

Gus: Do you want me to recite it word for word? Remember, I'm a—

Ellen: —genius...with feelings, no less.

Gus: What about it?

Ellen: Think.

(Gus closes his eyes and ponders Ellen's request. After a few minutes, he begins to nod.)

Gus: Page thirty-nine. Orv, my make-believe, supernatural foster father says: "You can't say hello..."
And then Jill, his wife, says: "...until you say goodbye."

Ellen: Yup. That's what it's all about. You can't say hello to something or someone until you've said goodbye. A kid whose mother angrily yells, *"Wait till I see you after school!"* as she drops him off in the morning, is not ready to say hello to his first class. He'll still be fussing with the goodbye. Similarly, a kid who suffers a messy rejection (in other words, a bad goodbye), is going to have trouble saying hello to the next one unless the old one is worked through.

Gus: I've been doing better here. They're talking about me leaving soon. Do you think I've worked through my good-byes?

(Ellen doesn't answer. An awkward silence envelops the room. A vacant gaze appears on Gus's face. A few minutes later, Gus speaks quietly.)

Gus: I couldn't handle being around Jay today. It hurt somethin' awful.

Ellen: I know.

Gus: Every ounce of me was crying out to connect with the folks I've lost. It was weird. For a while, I couldn't think about anything but my father. You know, I don't really know much about him.

Ellen: Do you want to learn more?

Gus: I don't know. He was a drug addict who overdosed on heroin. The dude must have been really fucked up. My mother said he suffered with depression, was extremely bright, and could be quite funny – when he was in the mood. I don't know much more.

Ellen: Maybe helping Jay will help you?

Gus: Maybe I should jump off a fuckin' bridge? I don't know if I want to deal with this crap. It hurts...and *I have* been doing better.

Ellen: Hey, not everyone has to go back and work through unfinished business. There are strategies to move us forward that don't involve revisiting issues in our past. C'mon, Mr. Genius, you've read some of the cognitive-behavioral books. You stole my article on solution-oriented possibility therapy. Sometimes we move forward by focusing on our strengths, seeing the positive side of things, reframing.

Gus: Like telling a tough kid that she's good at pushing people away instead of calling her obnoxious? Didn't you use that on me a few times?

Ellen: Precisely. Or, telling a kid who is upset, because a cherished staff member is leaving the program, that maybe the two of them were both incredibly lucky to have known each other; to value and focus on that instead of dwelling on the negative feelings the loss stirs up.

Gus: I guess when you've had a hard life it's easy to see the glass as always half-empty. We expect bad to happen and sometimes don't give positive thinking a chance.

Ellen: No one makes it through life without bad things happening. No one. Kids like you get more then they deserve. Kids who make it often do so because they have the ability to let go of negative, self-defeating thoughts and welcome new, more positive ways of understanding situations.

Gus: Hey, that's easy to say. It's nice psychological crap. But Juan's mother died of AIDS. His father has ALS and will be dead within a year. How does he deal with that? What hope do you give him? Should I tell him to think positively? Give me a fuckin' break.

Ellen: Hey, shit happens, Gus. Bad shit. But we've got choices in life. We all do. We can all choose to give up when life looks hopeless, or *choose* to find a way out of that deep hole we're in. I've chosen to help kids and families get out of those holes. And some do. The ones with guts.

Gus: Sounds great, Swamee. But I think you'll need a friggin' crane to pull Juan out.

Ellen: Juan will need to grieve and it won't be easy. But, at some point, it might help him to hear about kids who have lost both parents and made it in life - and there are lots of them; he needs to see that there *is* a possibility of being happy. If he loved his parents, and I think he did, then he can be counseled to cherish and rejoice in the relationship he enjoyed with both of them. And to not take that for granted. A relationship is like fuel. It can keep you going even when it's a memory. And there's always the snowball.

Gus: What?

Ellen: The snowball.

I tell kids who are dealing with a serious loss, or a fear of something – like being rejected, to imagine that their fear or emotional pain was like a large snowball embedded in their chest. I tell them, and I believe this, that every day that goes by the snowball will melt a little and that in time, it will become much smaller and manageable. It will never go away. But it won't compromise your life any more. Time helps the healing process.

Gus: I really miss my father. Do you think that's nuts?

Ellen: Not at all. It seems like you got a big snowball to deal with.

Gus: I got to say good-bye, don't I?

Ellen: Is what you're doing now working for you?

Gus: What do you mean?

Ellen: What do you think?

Gus: Christ, I hate when you say that.

(30 seconds of silence)

I'm getting by. I'm behaving better. I'm doing okay with my mom. I like being with Jay...

(10 seconds of silence)

Ellen: ...and?

Gus: And, I may need to do some more work around Daddio. I've kind of felt something weighing me down. Didn't know it was a freakin' snowball.

Shit, Ellen, Can't you use some of that positive thinking stuff on me? I'm not sure I want to go where this is heading.

Ellen: Why don't you think about this stuff some more and we'll talk again in a few days.

Gus: I'm beat.

Ellen: You did some good work today. I'm proud of you.

Man, that was a brutal get-together. I think I'm feeling even more messed up. I do, however, like when she says she's proud of me. Ellen means something to me, and that means her words carry a lot of weight. We don't often have folks stating they're proud of us. It feels good.

I think I'll go find a rock to crawl under.

4. Hellos and Goodbyes
Part Two

The next day I got a message that Ellen wanted to see me. I headed over to her office.

Ellen: How are you doing today?

Gus: I feel wacked out.

Ellen: I'll bet. Yesterday was heavy.

Gus: Why did you want to see me so soon?

Ellen: I've only got about ten minutes, but I wanted to tell you about Maria, a kid I worked with at my first residential center. Last night, I couldn't get her out of my mind as I thought about the talk we had. I think her story might be helpful to you.

Gus: Go for it.

Ellen: Maria – and that wasn't her real name - was a sweet, eleven-year-old kid who came to us from another program. One week before she was scheduled to leave her original program, to return home to her adoptive family, the family called and said they no longer wanted her. And no longer wanted any contact. These people had raised her since she was seven months old.

Everyone was devastated: Maria, the program, and her caseworker. It was decided that she would come to our center to live. She had apparently worn out her welcome at the first program.

I remember talking with her caseworker.

She was *furious* with Maria's family. According to her, they were the scum of the earth.

So, Maria comes to live with us. Right away it's obvious that she's a very challenging kid. Despite being sweet and lovable, she was highly disorganized, extremely messy, clumsy, hyperactive, and at times oppositional. A great kid but exhausting to work with.

She rarely mentioned her family. The subject was too painful.

After three or four months, I start thinking that maybe there was more here than meets the eye. Maybe Maria's adoptive family was getting a bad rap. Perhaps they got pressured to take her home...and agreed, even though they knew she was too tough to handle. After all, *we* were having trouble with the kid. And *we* were a top-notch residential program.

To make a very long story short, after consulting with our program director, I called Maria's caseworker in order to get permission to contact Maria's family. From a treatment perspective, I thought Maria was stuck and needed to work on her family issues. The caseworker refused our request. It really ticked her off that we wanted to reach out to them. *What kind of scum would abandon their kid two days before she was ready to return home for good? Forget about them,* was her message. But we couldn't, so I jumped rank and spoke to her supervisor. Eventually – and grudgingly – we were granted permission to speak with Maria's family. But there was a catch.

Maria's entire family was attending weekly therapy sessions to deal with the emotional upheaval caused by their decision. They would speak to us only with their therapist present. We agreed.

I remember entering their therapist's office for the first time. I saw Maria's mom and dad, and the sight broke my heart. Each was like a shell of a human being. The mom couldn't stop crying. Their guilt was palpable.

We had been correct.

A very loving family who had done their best for her had indeed raised this child. Maria was reportedly born with a host of neurological problems and her initial months of life were not warm and fuzzy – if you get my drift.

The family tried everything to help her function well in life, but it was always an uphill battle. As she got older, the problems mounted. Eventually, they had no choice but to place her in a residential treatment facility.

In residential care, she continued to prove difficult to manage. The program wanted her to return home – they had experienced enough – and pressured Maria's family to set a discharge date. The family didn't have the strength to tell the program or Maria that they weren't ready, and that they believed Maria wasn't ready.

A few days before they were supposed to bring Maria home, they called the program and said they couldn't do it. They knew they weren't ready. The decision psychology devastated them. I'm not sure they will ever be the same.

Along with my program director, we continued to meet monthly with Maria's family at their therapist's office. The meetings were terribly sad. But, eventually, we arrived at a good place.

The family decided that they could never have Maria return home on a permanent basis. However, they agreed to visit her four times a year at our program and kept open the possibility of more contact if things went well. The family had two biological children, a girl, 15 and a boy, 13. Maria had mentioned them to me. She missed her siblings *a lot*.

I'll never forget the day I brought Maria down to my office to inform her about all of this. She had no idea that the program director and I had been meeting with her family for months.

When I told her everything that was going on, she appeared somewhat stunned and then broke into tears. I sat down next to her and put my arm around her shoulders. After a few minutes, she looked up at me and said, *"I couldn't move forward until I saw my family."*

Those words flash in my head like a neon light:

I COULDN'T MOVE FORWARD UNTIL I SAW MY FAMILY

It's all about the hellos and goodbyes, Gus.

Gus: Did she see her family?

Ellen: Yeah, it was great. I remember it was a brisk October day. They came loaded with pictures and scrapbooks, letters from grandparents, and all the foods Maria liked. The initial hugs were hearty and long. We went through a lot of tissue that afternoon.

Gus: Did Maria do better after that?

Ellen: Yes she did.

I remember that she was selected to give the graduation speech at her special education high school. She delivered a very moving talk. Her entire family was in the audience. They were proud.

Gus: Jeez, that's one hell of a story. I can relate.

Ellen: I thought you would, my friend.

71

4. Hellos and Goodbyes
Part Three

(A few days later)

I've got a home visit scheduled for tomorrow. Things have been going pretty good between my mom and yours truly. I go home every weekend. I'm scheduled to go home for good at the end of the school year. We occasionally go at it, but we generally work our crap out.

I couldn't sleep last night. Kept thinking about Jay, the Brickmans, my dad, and Maria; that poor kid.

Most of the records at the Hills have been computerized. All reports are written on computers and sent to their rightful destinations. This makes data much easier to manage – and much easier to get at – if, you happen to be a computer geek, genius type, like the one and only me.

It just so happens that I snuck onto the computer at the front desk today and retrieved a little bit of information that I needed. The secretary, Mildred, has an irritable bowel condition – don't ask me how I know – so, she takes a lot of walks. Ol' Mildred also happens to be a big Tom Hanks fan, the movie star; she has a picture of him on her desk. Today, during one of her walks, I "borrowed" her computer. It didn't take long to figure out her password: Bosom Buddies. (An old sitcom Hanks was in.)

Once I logged on, it was only minutes before the information I sought appeared on the screen:

Fred and Carla Brickman
45 Wyman Street
Pareville, Connecticut

"BINGO!" I exclaimed.

Tomorrow, when mom picks me up, we're going to take the l-o-n-g way home.

(Next day...while driving home)

Mom: So how y'a been doing?

Gus: I've been feeling kind of screwy.

Mom: Why? What's up?

Gus: You know that I've been helping out with one of the new kids, Jay.

Mom: Yes, it sounded like a good idea.

Gus: Well, it hasn't been so easy. I thought it would be a piece of cake, but I was wrong. Talking with him has kicked up a lot of feelings and crap from my own life. The kid has been through hell.

Mom: Maybe you shouldn't work with him anymore?

Gus: Dammit, Ma. I think this kid needs me. The answer isn't to run away. Reject him like everyone has.

Mom: Don't get so uptight. I was just thinking about you.

Gus: *(angrily)* Were you thinking about me when you deserted me for five years, Ma?

(Gus's mother pulls the steering wheel hard to the

right, slams on the brake, and brings the car to a rest in the breakdown lane.)

Mom: What the heck is going on? We've been through this a million times. You know why I left, my problems with drugs – you know it all. I've apologized. We've talked about this in family therapy for close to a year. I've become someone you can trust. What is this all about?

Gus: I'm sorry. I'm all fucked up.

Mom: Do you have to swear?

Gus: Please, don't give me the language shit right now. I'm doing better with my mouth – but now's not the time, okay?

Mom: So what's up?

Gus: This kid, Jay, was supposed to get adopted by a family, the Brickmans. He lived there for almost a year. They accused him of touching a neighbor's kid's crotch, and booted him out of their home; they don't want him back. Don't even want to see him, and it's tearing the kid apart.

Helping him deal with this has evoked a wave of loss feelings in me; some that I thought I had buried. I've thought about you leaving me, some of the foster parents, my dad –

Mom: Your dad? You never knew him.

Gus: Yeah, but that doesn't mean I can't miss him...want to know more about him. He's part of me and I know so little about the

75

guy. You mentioned him in that letter you wrote me last year, but you haven't talked about him since. It's like the subject is taboo. That sucks.

Mom: I didn't want you to be hurt more.

Gus: Look, I've got a lot of questions about my father. There's a lot I want to know. But not right now.

(Gus takes a folded up piece of paper from his pocket. On the top of it is the word Mapquest*)*

At this moment, I'd like you to take these directions and get us to Pareville.

Mom: What are you talking about?

Gus: You heard me, Ma. We're going to Pareville. I want to talk face-to-face with the Brickmans.

Mom: Are you nuts? We can't show up unannounced at someone's house like that. Besides, you can't get involved in someone else's affairs. You don't have all the information. This isn't your business. There are trained professionals dealing with this.

Gus: The fuck it ain't my business.

Mom: Gus, we could get in big trouble. You're supposed to be discharged soon. How did you even get their address? On second thought, don't tell me.
Gus, we're not going and that's final. It's a crazy idea.

Gus: I know it's crazy, but I gotta do it.

Kids like Jay, like me, often go through life haunted by bad shit from our past. We have trouble saying hello to new relationships and situations because we're still fussing with so many bad goodbyes.

Ma, if you didn't come back into my life and help me make sense of why you left, I would have gone on the rest of my life blaming myself for the reason. And when you think you're bad it's pretty hard to sustain any new kind of relationship – cause you think once the person gets to know the real you, it's all over.

Whenever I got booted from a foster family, or whenever a staff member I liked left the program, I blamed myself. They all left or kicked me out because I was a bad kid. That's what your leaving taught me. When you came back and convinced me that I wasn't the reason, it was as if a hundred-pound weight was lifted off my shoulders. It freed me up to have the courage to trust people, to believe in myself.

Too many kids get booted from foster homes because of bad behavior and never hear from their foster parents again. As a consequence, these kids go through life scarred. Sure, we kids can be difficult to manage. But far too often the goodbyes aren't handled well. After a kid is booted from a family there should be meetings and letters between the kid and the family that help the kid understand that he or she was a great kid who simply needed more help than the family could offer. This just doesn't happen enough.

Ma, Jay is really hurting. I've walked in his shoes. I need to talk...I need to...

(Gus's mother goes into her pocketbook and takes out a small package of tissues. She gives a few to her son to help wipe away his tears.)

Mom: *(teary-eyed)* We can't do this Gus. We just can't...

Gus: *(in a choked-up voice)* Ma...please...

Mom: I said we can't do this...on an empty stomach. How about a few Big Macs and some fries first? Pareville is a three-and-a-half hour drive.

4. Hellos and Goodbyes
Part Four

Gus: Turn over there. That's Wyman Street.

Mom: Are you sure you want to do this? It will get us in trouble. Who knows, it might delay your return home?

Gus: I gotta do this, Mom.

Mom: Just answer me one question.

Gus: Shoot.

Mom: Are you doing this for the right reasons? Is this about helping Jay or helping Gus?

Gus: That was two questions.

Mom: Well?

Gus: I don't know. Maybe a little bit of both.

Mom: That's fair.

Gus: Pull the car over for a second.

(Gus's mom parks the car on the side of the road, two houses before the Brickmans.)

Mom: Having second thoughts?

(Gus remains silent for almost a minute; his mother can see that he's deep in thought. His face is solemn. His gaze is focused on the red jeep parked ahead. He finally speaks, but does not look at her.)

Gus: Ma, I'm only fourteen, but I'm smart and I think about things. I look around me every day and I see people, me included, functioning in our safe little comfort zones. It takes a lot of courage to step outside a zone; to enter the treacherous domain of the unpredictable. Like it or not, we all crave familiarity – or comfortability. In most cases, we'd rather stay inside and be unhappy than venture outside for happiness – because the risks are too great. *What if this happens? What if that happens? Will I fail? Will they like me? Can I do this?*

Ma, I bet a lot of folks look back at their lives and wish they had shown a little more courage...didn't let negative thinking bring 'em down... had stretched their comfort zones. Hindsight, after all, is twenty-twenty.

Today I'm stepping outside the zone and you're helping me take the steps.

(Gus's mom seems taken aback by her son's comments. She pauses before responding.)

Mom: Gus, that was impressive. Where did you learn to think like that?

Gus: I dunno. Maybe my dad was a deep thinker. Maybe that's why he offed himself. What do you think?

Mom: I think you and I need to talk more about your father. But right now we're parked two houses down from the Brickmans. Do you really want to do this?

Gus: No, I don't. But I'm not turning back. It's zone-stretching time. Hey, I'm scared about this. I bet the Brickmans are good people who went through hell with Jay. I'm not naive. They probably had excellent reasons for what they did. I just want them to do better with the goodbye.

Shoot. They'll probably be really pissed that I had the nerve to visit their home. This could get ugly fast.

Yup, there's a big part of me that wants to turn around and get the hell out of here.

But today I'm *going* to do something that will be very uncomfortable. I'm *going* to visit the Brickmans to try and help my friend Jay – and, hopefully, the Brickmans. I am *going* to step outside the zone.

Mom: Watch your step, son.

Gus: Thanks.

There's the house. Pull into the driveway.

(Gus gets out of the car and slowly walks up the front walk. He pauses before climbing the three badly cracked cement steps, and then proceeds. The doorbell is broken, seems smashed in. "Jay was here," Gus thinks to himself. After another interminable pause, Gus takes a quick glance at his mother and then knocks three times on the door. He hears movement in the house. "Damn, they're home," he nervously mutters.)

Fred: Hello. Can I help you?

Gus: Yes, you can. My name is Gus

Studelmeyer. I live at the Highland Hills Residential Treatment Center. I was asked a few months ago to act as a mentor to Jay Bloom, your former foster child.

Fred: Are you kidding me? You're from the center? How the hell did you get here? How did you get our name and address? This is ridiculous! Get out of here. *(with rising anger)* Haven't we been through enough?

(Mr. Brickman slams the door shut. Gus is somewhat stunned, but not terribly surprised. After a few seconds, he knocks again. After a short pause, a disturbed Fred Brickman opens the door.)

Fred: Look, pal, we don't want to talk to you. If you don't leave in three seconds I'm going to call your program and give them a piece of my mind. I'm then going to report you and that sorry agency to the Department.

(He slams the door shut again.)

Gus: *(loudly)* PLEASE let me in. I'll only stay for a few minutes. It's really important that we speak.

(Gus hears loud voices emanating from inside.)

Gus: *(even louder)* I'VE COME A LONG WAY. I'M DOING THIS FOR JAY. HE CRIED FOR

(No response from the Brickmans. Gus waits...and waits. He sits down on the top step and lowers his head. "Maybe this wasn't such a good idea," he utters to himself. After ten minutes, he gets up to leave. Suddenly, he hears the door crack open. A distraught Carla Brickman appears.)

Carla: Did you say Jay cried for us?

Gus: Yes I did. He misses you.

Carla: Did he send you hear to talk with us? Does he want you to convince us to take him back? Is that it?

(The door opens wider and Fred Brickman appears)

Gus: He doesn't know I'm here. For that matter, no one, besides my mother who's waiting in the car, *(Gus points to her)* knows I'm here.

Fred: Kid, you really caught us off guard. I'm sorry I lashed out at you. Jay's leaving has been hard on us. We're a bit frayed around the edges.

Gus: No problem. I thought you might be a tad upset to see me.

Carla: Do you always do this kind of thing?

Gus: No. I decided to stretch my comfort zone and give this a shot. I was pretty nervous about coming here.

Fred: *(smiling)* You've got big Kahoonas, my boy.

Gus: If that means what I think it means.
         Thank you.

Carla: Would you and your mother like to come
         in?

Gus: She's okay out there. She's always got a
         book or two under the seat. This should-
         n't take long.

Fred: Okay. Come on in.

(Gus is escorted in to the Brickman's living room.)

Carla: Would you like something to eat?

Gus: Thanks. But we just downed some Big
         Macs.

Fred: How's Jay?

Gus: He ain't doing too well. As I said, I think
         he misses you guys.

Fred: That's a bit surprising to hear.

Gus: Why?

Carla: Didn't he tell you what happened?

Gus: He said you accused him of touching one
         of the neighbor's kids in his private area.

Carla: He denied doing so?

Gus: He didn't say yes or no.

Fred: Gus, we know he touched our neighbor's
         son. The kid's mother caught him in the
         act. She was mortified. They've stopped
         talking to us and will probably file a law-
         suit.

Carla: We gave that kid everything we had, but
         his behaviors kept getting worse and
         worse. That was the only sexual acting
         out we knew about. I mean towards

another kid, but he often used sexual terms when angry with us, and he masturbated a lot.

Fred: Not always appropriately.

Carla: You wouldn't believe the things he said to us.

Gus: Yup. I would.

Fred: Look Gus, I understand you care about him. We had heard he was assigned a mentor. But I don't think it's right for us to get into specifics about what he did here. That's confidential material.

Carla: I will tell you this. When we confronted him about Zack, the neighbor's boy, he went ballistic. He ran around the house breaking things; some quite expensive, and then punched Fred in the face, almost broke his nose.

Fred: *"I hate you f—-in people."* He kept screaming. *"Get me out of this f—-in' house!"* We called the police. Had him removed.

Carla: Enough was enough. How much could we take? We know he had a horrible past, but he just wasn't ready to live here.

Fred: After all we did for him. To trash the house, punch me in the face, and yell how much he hates us...obviously he didn't want to be here. And frankly, that last day pissed us off so much, that it wasn't too hard to send him away. I'm still angry with the kid. I know he's got his reasons, he's troubled – but, man, he shouldn't have acted that way, not towards us.

Carla: It was probably a bad match. Maybe we were deluding ourselves thinking that he was beginning to attach to us. We're not sure he ever wanted to be with us.

Gus: He thought you might adopt him.

Fred: Yeah, we brought that up a few months ago. It was probably a mistake to have mentioned it. He only got worse afterwards.

Gus: I don't think it was a bad match. I think it was a great match. I think my little friend is very angry, very scared, and very confused. I don't know much about his early years. They must have been horrible. That's what his behavior is telling us. When I was younger, I was like Jay. I trusted no one. My mother, my relatives, they all hurt me, some in a sexual way. I grew up assuming that all adults were potential abusers. If a foster parent was nice to me, it made it even harder to be there. Because when he or she turned on me – and my caretakers always did, it would be even more painful to deal with.

Carla: Gus, why did you come here?

Gus: I didn't come to get you to reconsider taking Jay back. But I want you to help him say goodbye.

Fred: What do you mean?

Gus: The poor kid thinks you don't like him anymore. He thinks you view him as a bad kid. He probably feels terrible about his actions on the last day. It will be easier for him to say hello to a new family if you can help him say goodbye to you folks and what he had here. If you don't, he'll go through life weighed down by this experience. His feeling of being a loser – which I'm sure he had well before he entered your home – will only be reinforced.

Fred: I don't know if I'm ready to see him.

Carla: Those last few days were pretty traumatic.

Gus: I hear you. I'm not saying to march right over to the center and talk this through with him. Do it when you're both ready. But you gotta do it. Please, don't leave the kid hanging in the wind. I really think he loves you guys.

Fred: Hey, you're laying quite a guilt trip on us. Look at my wife. You've made her cry.

(Carla's face is again buried in a tissue.)

What about us, Gus? Is this all about Jay?

Carla: *(in a stern, dispassionate tone)* Maybe you should go. I'm suddenly feeling like a very bad parent.

Fred: Don't go there, Carla. You gave that kid everything you had. He wasn't ready to be here. We've talked and talked and talked about this.

Carla: So, Gus, do you think all foster parents

like screwing kids? Are we just in it for the money?

Fred: Honey. Cut it out.

Carla: No, I want to hear what he has to say.

Gus: I didn't come hear to hurt your feelings.

Carla: But you came here thinking we're another set of foster parents who don't care enough to hang in there with a kid, or say "goodbye" properly. That's what you thought, right?

Gus: No. I didn't think that.

Carla: Bullshit! I can see it in your eyes. You had us judged. Well, the hell with you. I loved that kid. Still do. But we just couldn't take it anymore. He hurt us bad.

I can't have kids. Jay was going to be our son. A day doesn't go by that I don't think about what we could have done differently. So listen, you can take your holier-than-thou attitude and leave right now. I've heard enough.

Fred: Gus, you better leave.

(Gus gets up and heads for the door. After four or five steps, he stops and looks at the couple.)

Gus: Wait. Please don't make me leave like this.

You're right. I did come here with a chip on my shoulder. I did prejudge you. I'm truly sorry. The only foster parents I ever knew all booted me from their homes. Some of them hurt me. I guess I'm somewhat jaded.

Fred: Thank you for that. Most foster parents really do care about their kids. When it's not working, it hurts like hell. Goodbye, Gus. And thanks for helping Jay.

(Gus is escorted to the front door. He solemnly descends the front steps and heads for his car. Halfway to the vehicle, he hears Carla yell to him. She's running in his direction)

Carla: I'm sorry I lost my cool back there. Please forgive me.

(Gus could see that she had done a lousy job wiping away her tears. The moment hit him hard. He stepped forward, paused and hugged her. He didn't want to go.)

Gus: *(in a hushed tone)* Thanks.

(Gus slowly retreats and strolls to the car, his back to Carla.)

Carla: Wait.

(Gus turns in her direction.)

    Did he *really* cry for us? He always held in his feelings.
Gus: Yeah. He did.
Carla: Well, I guess that's something.

(Gus moves closer to her.)

Gus: Look, I still think the goodbye stuff is important, but so is all the time he spent with you. Not many people would have hung in there with him as long as you two did. Down the road, he'll be better off because of your efforts.

Carla: Do you really think so?

Gus: Yeah. I do.

Carla: Thanks.

(Gus turns and walks towards the car. Carla runs to him and plants a soft kiss on his cheek)

          Have a good life, Gus. And take care of our boy.

Gus: Consider it done.

(Gus enters his mom's car. Two seconds after fastening the seat belt, he whips it off, jumps from the car and yells to Carla, who had almost disappeared inside her house.)

Gus: Hey!

Carla: What?

Gus: *(yelling)* Ah, maybe you don't have to tell anyone that we came by?

(Carla gazes in Gus's direction, smiles, and then yells back)

Carla: Consider it done.

(Gus gets into his mother's car.)

Mom: Well?
Gus: It went okay. Do you mind if we don't talk
          about it right now?
Mom: No problem.

(Gus spent a quiet weekend with his mother. He felt drained. He wasn't up for any ghost hunting)

4. Hellos and Goodbyes
Part Five

(Jay had the flu the following week. Two weeks later they met for their fourth meeting.)

Place: Basketball court.

Gus: How's it going?

Jay: Okay.

(Jay picks up the basketball and begins shooting.)

Gus: Are you over the flu?

Jay: Yeah, I'm okay.

(The two boys shoot quietly for a few minutes.)

Jay: *(in a muted tone)* I made level two this week.

Gus: *(very animated)* Hey, that's great! Slap me five, buddy!

(Gus extends his flat palm to Jay. Gus sees Jay's hand start to raise, but he quickly pulls it back and resumes shooting)

Gus: Level two means you earn some fun privileges.

Jay: Yeah, whatever.

Gus: Hey, maybe you're not too excited, but I think it's fantastic. It took me at least three months to earn some of those privileges.

Jay: Levels are dorky. I think it's stupid that they make you earn them.

Gus: I hear some programs don't use level systems.

Jay: Really?

Gus: Yeah. Some don't use 'em at all, and some do it day-to-day. Whatever points a kid earns on a given day are traded for things or privileges on the next day. That's it, no levels. More immediate.

Jay: I'd like that better.

Gus: Yeah, sometimes it seems kind of nutty that a kid who works months to earn a real high level could lose it – just like that – for one big screw-up. Puts a lot of pressure on the staff, too.

And with levels, if a kid has a really bad day, his week can be shot. It won't matter how he does the next few – because a high level is already out of reach. Kids lose their incentive.

Jay: Why can't they just give you the privileges if you can handle them? Why do you gotta earn everything?

Gus: Good questions, my man. They probably should do just that. Give kids any privilege that they could handle, but only let them use the privileges if their behavior is okay. Kind of what a family does.

Jay: Levels are stupid.

Gus: Look, man, I think they have to use

something to control us. Let's face it, we all come in angry and ready to rumble. We don't trust anyone. These folks need to have some goodies in place, some things we can earn, to help with our behavior. We're certainly not going to behave because someone we don't know or trust asks us to. Right?

Jay: Whatever.

(Gus and Jay shoot around for another 10 minutes.)

Gus: Okay, man, I think we need to wrap it up.

(As if he were waiting for these words, Jay immediately reaches into his back pocket and retrieves a folded up piece of paper. He approaches Gus.)

Jay: I got this last week.

(Jay hands Gus the wrinkled paper. Gus reads it.)

It was a letter to Jay...

Dear Jay,
We both hope you are doing well. We miss you. You are a fantastic kid! Your last few days with us were very difficult. You made some mistakes, and maybe we did, as well. We forgive you for all that happened.
We know there's no such thing as a bad kid; just kids who make bad choices now and then – probably because of the bad luck they've had.

During your last few months, you made your share of bad choices. You were letting us know that life was really hard for you. Maybe we should have done a better job listening and figuring out what to do.

Jay, we don't want you to ever think we kicked you out. You just needed more help then we could give. Highland Hills is a place that can provide this help…if you let them.

When we think about you, we don't dwell on the last few days; instead, we remember the time we all went to the beach and you flew your kite higher than anyone, and how we chowed down on three-pound lobsters afterwards. Boy, that was a fun day!

We remember tucking you in each night and telling goofy bedtime stories. Cooking eight-inch wide chocolate chip cookies. Spending all day digging out a vegetable garden and planting a half-dozen Azalea bushes. We sure got dirty, didn't we?

And we'll never forget the food fight. Wasn't that a riot? The three of us buried under whipped cream and chocolate sauce!

Despite all that happened, we both feel incredibly lucky that we got to be a part of your life. You are a very special kid.

It hurts us bad to say that we can't be your family any more. We wish we could take away all the bad things that happened to you earlier in life; all the bad luck. But we can't, and you need to work through some things, and where you are is the place to do it.

When you've done the work, and it will be hard – but we know you can do it - a new and very lucky family will be found for you. They will welcome a superstar, you, into their home. And you will grow up and do great things. We know it.

Within a month, we plan on seeing you at the program for a final visit. It will be a very hard day for us, and I guess for you. But we want to say good-bye face to face, and make sure you believe the things we've said in this letter. We'll bring some of your favorite pictures and other odds 'n ends you left behind.

Take care, pal.

Love,

Carla and Fred

(Gus finishes reading the letter. It moves him. He looks at Jay who is staring intently into his eyes.)

Jay: They don't hate me, do they?

Gus: No, I guess not.

Jay: Maybe I don't have to hate them?

Gus: You could probably think about letting that feeling go.

Jay: I wish I were still with 'em.

Gus: I don't blame you. It sucks that it didn't work out. Sucks royally. But they're right. Some family is going to be lucky to get you.

Jay: I got to go. My counselor is here.

Gus: Be good, dude.

The Brickmans came through. I think Jay will be able to move forward now. It won't be easy. But he's a tough little guy, and I think he's got the guts to do the work. I think I'll call my mom and thank her again for taking me there. She came through, too. Damn, that's nice to think about.

5. Sex, Drugs, Friends, and Prejudice

I just got back from school and notice there's a letter on my bed. Cool. I don't get letters often; it's a rush. The return address has a familiar name scribbled on the top: Escavez

"A letter from Hector!" I yell excitedly. I haven't seen the dude in two years. As noted in Gus I, Hector was my first best friend. Man, did we do some crazy shit together.

Hate to admit it, but we weren't always kind to new staff, especially if they started with an attitude. One prick named Chuck really had a hair up his butt. He liked to be "da man," a real power guy. He worked at another program before coming to the Hills and thought he knew it all. We hated that.

Two to three weeks after he entered the scene, I approached ol' UpChuck (as Hector and I affectionately called him).

Gus:	Hey Chuck, do you want to hear something interesting?
Chuck:	Yeah, why not?
Gus:	Hector's father is a zoologist.
Chuck:	What's that?
Gus:	He studies animals. In fact, he's currently living at the South Pole studying polar bear behavior. He actually killed one with a jack knife.
Chuck:	Are you kidding me?
Gus:	No. He's been published. You can read some of his research.
Chuck:	Bet he never killed a polar bear. Probably

said that to impress his kid. I got to go.

(Later that night, Chuck approached Hector.)

Chuck: Hey, I heard where your father lives. I think it's great.

Hector: *(Aghast and bug-eyed)* You think it's great?

Chuck: Yeah.

Hector: *(screaming, agitated)* YOU THINK IT'S GREAT, MAN!

Chuck: *(confused)* Yes I do. And I think the animal thing, as well as his writing is also cool.

Hector: *(with a sad, stilted delivery)* My fa...my father...is locked up...locked up in prison for shooting a donkey. His writing hand, the left one, was blown off during a fourth of July celebration. He can't write any-more. Why do you taunt me? *(crying)* You are a mean man. A MEAN MAN!

(Hector begins running through the residence screaming)

"PAPA! PAPA! PAPA!............

"HE DIDN'T SHOOT THE DONKEY!

"HE DIDN'T SHOOT THE DONKEY!"

I thought Chuck was going to drop a load in his pants. If there had been any kind of hole in the floor, he would have found a way to shrivel up and crawl into it.

We were better to him, afterwards. Turns out, he wasn't such a bad guy. Guess he came on strong to hide his insecurity. Guess that's not unusual. Pittsiotti, the Director, had Hector and me doing work programs for two weeks to pay for this prank. It was worth it.

Ah, Hector. I miss you, buddy. We took care of each other. We shared things. We were brothers. I excitedly opened the letter. Hey, maybe he'll be visiting soon. I took the letter out. The handwriting wasn't Hector's. That seemed strange. I began reading...

Dear Gus,

I hope you are doing well. Your friendship with my son was a special gift. You were his amigo; he loved you. I am sorry to have to tell you that Hector is dead. He died last week from injuries suffered in a beating. The police still aren't sure who did it. They think it might have been a group of kids from the homeless shelter Hector had stayed at.

Gus, Hector was gay. He was building up the courage to tell you. He wasn't sure how you'd take the news. He came out a year ago.

After he disclosed his homosexuality, kids at school made life miserable for him. They teased him real bad. They called him a fag, a fruit, a femme, and a bunch of other names I'm too uncomfortable to write. They glued his locker shut, roughed him up, and wrote things on the school walls that devastated him. He'd often return home trembling and in tears. My heart ached for him.

"Why, Mama does being gay bother them so much?"

"Why can't they leave me alone?"

He'd repeat these questions over and over. They never let up. I heard from a parent of a gay son, that teenagers who come out can expect to be teased or taunted at least two dozen times every day. Why do kids have to be so damn mean?

He didn't feel bad about being gay. He was proud of who he was. But he did have second thoughts about coming out. Life was never the same. He felt very alone. It was so hard to watch this happening; I felt helpless.

As the months went by, I started to lose him. He turned to drugs, grass at first, then cocaine and, I think, Oxycontin. It was his escape. During the summer, he had earned almost two thousand dollars helping a landscaper; he spent it all on drugs. He had been saving the money so that we could buy a car.

Gus, he knew doing drugs was wrong. One night, after we had argued about his drug problem, he broke down and cried. Through his tears, he said "Mama, I know these drugs are eating away at my brain, but the pain is just so bad. It's the only way I can escape. Help me, Mama."

The next day, I brought him to a drug rehab program. They helped him. He really did have the courage to stop using. But as soon as he returned to school, it started all over again; the teasing, the taunting, the incessant ridicule. The poor kid would come home a shell of himself.

I complained to his principal. He said he'd try and help. I don't think he did a damn thing. I got the impression that he was uncomfortable with Hector being openly gay. I think he wished that Hector would just disappear; and that's exactly what he did. He ran away three months ago. I didn't see him again until the hospital called and told me he was in a coma clinging to life, the victim of a brutal beating.

I've since learned that Hector ran to Boston. I got a call recently from a kid named Jessie; he told me what Hector's last few months were like. Jessie was also gay and a runaway. They met at a homeless shelter. They were going out together.

Gus, I haven't told anyone what Jessie said. I haven't even wanted to think about it. I cry and cry when I let myself picture my sweet Hector alone and afraid on the streets of Boston. I think I'm writing this to you to help me deal with the pain. Maybe I shouldn't. Maybe this isn't fair to you. But there is a part of me that thinks it's right for you to know.

To make money Hector did sexual things for men. Some would rough him up. He told Jessie that he was saving the money to help me buy a car, that he had blown his summer savings on drugs and wanted to make it up to me. But some of the money went for drugs.

Hector liked to look feminine. Sometimes he'd put on make-up and wear women's clothing. He said it made him feel comfortable. He knew I had a hard time with it, although I was working hard to accept it. I'd tell him "Hector, you've always been beautiful on the inside, it's just taking me some time to accept you being beautiful on the outside."

Maybe if I had been more accepting from the start he'd still be with us. At first, we fought a lot when he started dressing feminine. It was hard to deal with. It's not what I dreamed about when I first became a mother.

But after he came home a few times in tears, having been physically and emotionally roughed up a school, I could only see the inside - the beautiful young man I was proud to call my son.

God, he was such a special kid. When my mother took ill, he'd bring her flowers every day. He'd sit and read her stories, help her go to the bathroom and change, cook her meals. How many fifteen-year-old kids would do that? And she didn't care if he was gay or how he looked. Before she got really sick, they'd take turns making each other up.

Jessie told me not to blame myself for Hector running. He said that Hector loved me and wanted to return home. Jessie said he wished his parents were as understanding. They kicked him out, said he humiliated and disgraced them. I know dealing with a gay child is hard thing, but how can parents turn on their own flesh and blood? That isn't right.

I had his body cremated. I spread his ashes in the woods near our house. He loved it there. We had a simple ceremony. The priest said some nice things about him. I still can't believe he's gone. I'm not sure I'll ever be the same. He was my only child. It's hard to get through the day. I'm sorry this letter is filled with such sadness. It was all so unnecessary. There are too many gay kids up in heaven, Gus. Hector loved life. He loved you. Thank you for being his friend.

Love,
Carmalita Escavez

(After reading the letter, Gus slumps on his bed. He can't talk... think...or move. Seconds later, he's sobbing. Tears fall on the letter and blur some of the words. He rocks back and forth, shaking his head in utter disbelief.)

"No, no, no, ...Hector can't be dead. This isn't real.
Not Hector.
Not that way. Oh, God, make this go away."

(Gus wraps both hands around his midsection and rocks even harder. His sobs grow louder as he starts to pound his right foot violently against the floor. After a minute or two, he stops, rises, and yells with a dark, menacing scowl.)

"Appelstein! Get the fuck over here, you fucking asshole!"

(No response)

"Appelstein, come now or I don't write anymore!"

Appelstein:	Look, you're fictitious and I'm real. I told you in the first book that conversing with you is kind of weird.
Gus:	Why'd you do it?
Appelstein:	Do what?
Gus:	Don't give me that shit. You killed off Hector. The only real friend I ever had.
Appelstein:	I made Hector up. I made you up. Cool down, Bud.

Gus:	Fuck you! I feel real. I seem real to people. Don't throw this make-believe crap at me.
Appelstein:	All right. I'll play along. I killed Hector to make a point.
Gus:	What? That gay kids have it bad?
Appelstein:	As a matter of fact: yeah, that's why I did it.
Gus:	Tough man! Went out on a limb, eh?
Appelstein:	What's your point?
Gus:	Here's the point, Jack: You didn't take any chances with the Hector stuff. It was a safe little chapter. You got people feeling bad for gay kids. Threw in a little drug stuff. So what? It was vanilla writing.
Appelstein:	What does that mean?
Gus:	You are one dense guy.
Appelstein:	You don't have to get personal.
Gus:	Yes I do. This *is* personal. *Very personal* So, there's prejudice against gays. And more prejudice against male homosexuals who act and/or dress feminine. And drugs are bad. None of this is news, pal.
Appelstein:	Hey, I think it's worth writing about.
Gus:	*Please*...give it a rest.
Appelstein:	So what should I have written?
Gus:	In this book or the first one?
Appelstein:	Either one. Go ahead; enlighten me.

Gus:	Well, maybe in Gus I, you should have made me gay. Or had a gay character. Why didn't you?
Appelstein:	To be honest, it never entered my mind.
Gus:	And why is that?
Appelstein:	I don't know.
Gus:	Bullshit! That's no answer. I'll ask you again, why no gays in the first book?
Appelstein:	I told you, *I don't know!*
Gus:	You're getting upset, dude? What gives?
Appelstein:	I'm not-
Gus:	Here's why you didn't... It would have made you uncomfortable. You haven't worked with many gay kids. Heck, you don't even know many gay people. It was *easier* and more *comfortable* for you to make me a likable heterosexual, living in a likable, drug-free heterosexual environment. Sure, we wrote some good stuff in the first book. I'm proud of it. But maybe it could have been better. Maybe you didn't take enough risks.
Appelstein:	That's redicu-
Gus:	If you had made me gay and really explored the subject, I bet you would have worried about people questioning your sexuality; might

have worried that fewer people would want to read it.

Appelstein: That's crazy.

Gus: Hey, big guy, it was manlier to write *Gus* the way you did. You didn't have to move outside your comfort zone. It was safe writing. And, as a result, you turned your back on kids who really needed the help. That's a damn shame.

Appelstein: Most of the kids I've worked with have been straight. Gus (you) was created to be a *typical* kid in residential care.

Gus: So you had *me* (through you) write a whole freakin' book without shedding light on the excessive prejudice suffered by so many kids because of their sexual orientation and life-styles. You shut 'em out. Damn, I feel like a traitor.

Appelstein: I swear it wasn't intentional.

Gus: After you/I wrote the first Gus, I bet you looked back and realized you hadn't even broached the subject of homo- and trans- sexuality, or the drug stuff. You probably said to yourself *"Hey man, I better have Gus write about this stuff or people will think I'm uncomfortable with the subject areas."* After all, there are lots of hurtin' kids out there who are gay and/or transsexual,

	and others struggling with their sexuality; and lots of kids trying to cope with drug and alcohol problems.
Appelstein:	As a matter of fact, I did do that.
Gus:	So, you're trying to look cool by giving lip service to these subjects in *Gus II*.
Appelstein:	I'm not trying to look cool. I don't have expertise in every area of youth care. But I'm trying hard to cover all the bases. In *Gus II*, I'm trying to fill some gaps. The goal is to get people thinking about this stuff. You and I don't have to provide all the answers.
Gus:	Bullshit! Admit it. You like dealing with kids who are straight rather than homosexual. It would bother you to be surrounded by gay kids. A cross-dressing teen would be hard to deal with. You want to be around kids that are like you: White and heterosexual.
Appelstein:	The hell I do! You're way off base.
Gus:	Am I? If you were back working as a program director, at your last residential center, and one of your residents, an older teen, was gay and had a boyfriend, would you be comfortable dealing with it? What if the kid also had a crush on you? Over the years, some of the girls

did (and it never bothered you).
Well?

(No response)

Hello, Mr. Charlie...

(No response)

Earth to Appelstein...come in Appelstein.

(No response)

Appelstein:	Okay. It would make me feel uncomfortable to deal with the stuff you mentioned.
Gus:	Bingo. Now we're getting somewhere. You're homophobic.
Appelstein:	Knock it off. Being uncomfortable doesn't mean I'm homophobic.
Gus:	Call it what you want. But if a guy like you, one who lectures and writes books about troubled kids, has these issues, what about everyone else? I think the prejudice that many workers feel towards troubled kids is palpable. It can be because of their behavior, skin color, sexual orientation, or drug and alcohol histories – just to name a few. And you can slice it with a knife. But few admit it, think about it, and are forced to

confront it. And we kids pay for this indifference.

If people like you continue to deny that these attitudes exist, you remain part of the problem.

Appelstein: Do you want me to fall on a sword or something?

Gus: Don't get flip. I just don't want us writing through rose colored glasses anymore. There are many layers to prejudice. Chuck, you've got to reach deeper in these books, and in your work. Prejudice is like a cancer. You can't always see it – but it will get you if it's not addressed.

Appelstein: I hate when you call me Chuck.

Gus: I hate that Hector was killed. I hate that kids who are overweight, gay, transsexual, Hispanic, African-American, unattractive, short, yada, yada, yada...are treated unfairly every day by adults, like you, who think they are not prejudiced.

Appelstein: That's a strong statement.

Gus: Do you think that there are many youth care workers that would admit to favoring good-looking kids?

Appelstein: Not many.

Gus: Yet, I bet most of them do. And most aren't even aware they're doing it. I've seen it for years. Two kids have a borderline (not the diagnosis) type of day. The good-looking kid always seems to earn the higher level. Staff members generally gravitate towards the cute, attractive kids. Unattractive kids don't get as much attention. Been there/done that, Chuck.

Hey, you guys are just mirroring society. Let's face it, they don't put chubby kids like me in GAP commercials. Yet we're just as damn beautiful. Maybe more.

Appelstein: Man, I feel like I've been run over by a bulldozer. I've got a lot to think about.

Gus: Good.

Appelstein: I really do work hard to treat all kids with respect. I think about my feelings and possible prejudices when approaching a kid or uncomfortable situation.

Gus: I hope you do. But you've got to do even better. Don't get me wrong. I like what we wrote in the first Gus book. I think some of this lashing out at you is anger about Hector's death.

Appelstein: He was your friend. You haven't had many. You were like brothers.

Gus: Did you have to kill him?

Appelstein: I thought it made for a more pow-

	erful impact.
Gus:	C'mon...that's bulldung. The story wouldn't lose "impact" if you kept him alive in a coma. Why not give us some hope, man?
Appelstein:	I can't do that.
Gus:	Why? Because it would be cheap fuckin' sentimentalism. What? You're afraid of being criticized for not being tough enough?
	Man, it's easy for you to write this shit, play with my life – but I live with this pain.
Appelstein:	You're not real.
Gus:	*The hell I'm not!*
Appelstein:	What are you talkin' about?
Gus:	Do you think adults are the only people who read these books?
Appelstein:	No. A lot of kids do.
Gus:	You didn't think they would, did you?
Appelstein:	No.
Gus:	You had me write Gus I for professionals in the field. It never crossed your mind that kids who've had it rough would be reading and benefiting from Gus.
Appelstein:	No, it didn't.
Gus:	But they do. And as we write this book, you've had that in your mind, right?
Appelstein:	Yeah.
Gus:	Well, fart-breath, every time a

113

	courageous kid, whose had some real bad luck in life, sits down to read Gus, he or she *is* Gus. There's nothing fictitious there. It's the real deal. You got it?
Appelstein:	What's your point?
Gus:	What's your goal here?
Appelstein:	I guess it's to enlighten folks about kids and families who've had it rough.
Gus:	And that's narrow.
Appelstein:	Narrow?
Gus:	If we were writing this book only for adults, maybe that would fly. But when a kid sits down to read this, he or she might be looking for more than just enlightenment. Maybe the kid wants or needs some words of hope, and a few good feelings built in. What's so wrong about that? Who wants to see only movies with sad endings? Maybe you need to rethink this hard-hitting realism you're so proud of. Not worry about what "people" will think.
Appelstein:	What? You want me to keep Hector alive so that kids who read this book feel better?
Gus:	Yeah, that's it. We know all about pain, loneliness, sexual confusion, prejudice, abuse, rejection, etc. We're less familiar with feeling

| | good, okay Mr. Charlie? |
| Appelstein: | I can't give in like that. |

(With an anxious, bewildered expression)

WHAT ARE YOU DOING?

(Gus grabs Appelstein by the collar.)

	This can't be happening. You're fictitious.
	Let me go. GET OFF!
Gus:	*(face-to-face, two inches apart, with a measured rhythm and immense intensity)* I want you to bring Hector back. I don't want him to die. There aren't many people in this world who have loved me; he's one of 'em – and you can't kill him. You got that?
	This is a puny little book. That's all it is. But real people read it. Real people walk away with feelings. Maybe you should think about that a little more.
Appelstein:	Oh God, I'm must be suffering a breakdown.
Gus:	Bring Hector back.
Appelstein:	No. I can't do it. It would be selling out.

(Gus delivers a quick punch to Appelstein's midsection. He doubles over, gasping for air. Gus bends

down to continue the conversation.)

Gus: You breathin' yet?

(No reply from Appelstein)

> I'm sorry. I got carried away. I want to see my best friend again. That's all.
> In the real world, it takes a lot of hard work to make things better. I know that. But this story is all in your head. I know that, too.
> I don't want to go to bed tonight by crying myself to sleep - again. It's hard enough for me to drift off. I still have nightmares and worry whether I'll be safe at night...

(Gus begins to cry.)

> I just thought that maybe...

(Tears well in Appelstein's eyes.)

Gus: *(with an astonished expression)* Are those tears I see?

Appelstein: Yeah, you jerk. You broke me down.

(After a prolonged silence, Gus and Charlie connect with a hug.)

(The next day)

Dr. P.:	Gus, I've been looking all over the campus for you.
Gus:	What's up?
Dr. P.:	We received this urgent telegram twenty minutes ago. It's addressed to you.

(Gus anxiously opens the message and reads.)

Dear Gus,
It's a miracle! Hector is ALIVE!
He's still in a coma, but he's alive. It's a long story, but apparently there was a mix-up at the hospital. They cremated a cadaver.
Praise be the Lord! Hector is alive! There is hope!
Love,
Carmalita Escavez

(A big smile and a few big tears make their way to Gus's face.)

Gus:	Ah, yes, there's always hope. Thanks, dude.
Appelstein:	No, thank you, bud.

6. Structure, Structure, Structure:– But Don't Forget the Jokes!

It's been three weeks since I got the telegram from Hector's mother. The poor kid is still in a coma. But he's alive, and I got a feeling he's going to wake up one of these days. And when he does, this world better start treating him right.

I've seen Jay a few more times. He's doing okay; some weeks good, some weeks not-so-hot. That's the way it is with us kids. Once we taste a little success, we get worried and need to test things out a bit.

This past week, Jay needed to be held again. I think the little dude is worried stiff about the goodbye meeting with the Brickmans. They're coming in two weeks. That's a lot to handle. I've tried to talk with him about it, but he really doesn't want to go there. Actually, he *does* want to go there, but it's just too loaded for him.

Two weeks ago I visited with him on his unit. He punched a kid the day before and was restricted to his living space. Jay resides with thirteen other kids ages 5-12. Man, it brought back memories seeing that place. Most of all was the *structure, structure, structure.* There was structure up the wazoo:

Please sit here....line-up there...
Make sure you fold your underwear.
Dinner at five,
Bedtime at nine,
And make sure that your faces shine.
No swearing, farting, hitting, or teasing
And we'll call the nurse if you're wheezing.

119

Young, troubled kids (and even old dudes like me) need a lot of structure. In other words: predictability, sameness, consistency, routine: Got it? We always worry about *what's gonna happen next*. We're often on edge. The more structured a program is, the more we can relax and get some work done. Some of us have never lived in an environment that did it the same way every day – or at least tried.

If you want to help kids with mucho problems, you got to know structure. What does a structured environment look like? In my little ditty above, I noted some of the elements. Here's a few more. (I won't go overboard, here. I don't want to put y'all to sleep).

Structure, my friends, is:

Fooling around in the back of a movie theater with a hot babe!

(Nah, that's not structure...that's stature...I couldn't resist.)

Structure is:

Making sure the place always looks neat:

A messy environment will cause us to act messy. I always did better in settings that were run by neat-nicks – as long as the neat-nicks were humans, too (as opposed to Drill Sergeants). I remember living on a unit that was having a lot of problems – mucho physical restraints. A new unit director, Laura, took over and all she did was clean and paint...clean and paint. We asked her, "Why you cleaning so much?" She said, "Because how this place looks is a refection of how much we care about you guys." I haven't forgotten those words.

Transition times that are conducted well:

It's all about the hellos and good-byes. The younger and more troubled the group, the tighter staff should be around transitions. When I was a little whipper-snapper, if the staff didn't line us up properly and make sure we walked slowly and calmly to the next activity, we'd often get into heavy doo-doo. Every time we went anywhere, we were asked to sit quietly on a bench and the staff would review expectations for the transition. If we blew it and didn't walk calmly, the good staff made us return to where we started and try all over again.

Meals, groups, activities, bedtime, etc. that are generally at the same time each day:

Can you imagine being told every day when you had to eat, sleep, play, and bitch with your friends? If the times changed every day - you'd hate it. Well, welcome to our world, dude. Set times give us more control.

Rules that are fair and consistently applied:

Nothing ticks us off more than being treated unfairly. A place has to be tight in this area; but that doesn't mean overdo it. A kid came here recently and told us that his last residential program had 67 rules posted on the walls. Give me a break. Who the hell could remember 67 rules? Halfway through a shower, I can barely remember whether I shampooed my hair. I think some programs are so worried, so insecure, about handling kids like us that they try to come up with rules for every little behavior. Can't be done, Jack.

Unfortunately, some programs don't see the forest for the trees. They overdo the structure thing; they forget that we're just kids and not military dweebs. Yes, structure is critical but so is laughing (i.e. humor). The best residential programs and foster homes know how to properly mix the two.

I can remember too many occasions where a staff member started to joke with us and another staff told him or her to stop: *"Knock it off, I just quieted them down. Don't get 'em going."* I hate that line! *"Don't get 'em going."* Where the hell do they think we'll go? C'mon, some of us live in locked facilities!

This is an all points bulletin. Repeating. This is an all points bulletin. Little Johnny Applegate, from the ABC group home on Elmira, was told a joke at approximately 7:43am. He has not, I repeat, NOT, been able to stop going since the joke was told. Little Johnny, who also goes by the name Two-Fisted Willy, was last seen crossing the Nevada border. He has two arms, is laughing, and should not be considered dangerous. If you see the cute little fella, please bring him back to his group. Over and out.

"Don't get 'em going." Wrong. Get us going! We usually settle down for the staff members who use humor – because if we don't, they might get serious on us.

Programs always teach new youth care counselors how to set limits with, talk to, and restrain us dudes...but they rarely ever teach new staff how to make us laugh. That's awful. If I ran one of these places, a new worker would get two things on their first day of work: a handbook and a joke book. I would force them to be funny, particularly the shy, boring types.

When a staff member tells me to do something – and I generally don't like being told what to do – the first thought that enters my mind is: *Who is this jerk telling me what to do?* If the person is someone I like, someone who makes me laugh (the two are intimately connected), I'm more likely to do what he/she is asking. Humorous staff members have it much easier in this business, as long as they possess reasonable childcare skills.

Yesterday I dusted off my tape recorder and roamed the campus. I asked some of the staff members to relate funny episodes from their days in residential care. I heard some good ones. When I was done, I felt even more passionate about this subject. Here's some of what I heard.

Carl Venturo (Caucasian Unit Director/Adolescent Cottage)

"Two years ago I entered the cottage and heard ranting and raving coming from one of the bedrooms. I asked the senior counselor what was going on. She told me that Jessie, a large, tough African American kid with a history of gang involvement, was freaking out in his room because he wasn't allowed to go on the activity trip. He hadn't earned the right level.

"I walked down and entered his room. He saw me

and yelled, 'Get out of here, Carl. You're a racist! Get out of my room. You're a *racist! A racist!*'

I looked him in the eye and responded, 'I am *not* a racist. I hate all kids the same!' After a short pause, I cracked a smile and Jessie started laughing. We were pretty tight after that.

"Eight months later I'm walking through the mall with my wife and kid, and I notice Jessie up ahead with two of his buddies. I run up behind him, poke my finger in his back, and remark, 'Go ahead, make my day.' He whips around, sees me, and yells, 'Carl! My man! Remember the day I called you a racist? Do you still hate everyone the same, bro?' We shared a good laugh."

Vicky Kentock (Assistant Program Director)

"I had an angry seven-year-old boy in my office. He had just committed an inappropriate act and needed to process it with me. He wasn't cooling down too well. He tried to provoke me, saying 'This place sucks and you're an asshole.' I ignored him and went about my business.

"Noticing a picture of my husband and daughter, he remarked, 'Your husband is a dick and your daughter is a dog.' I continued to ignore him.

"He tried harder. Noticing a cross hanging on the wall (we were a religious organization), he proclaimed, 'And there is no God!' Hearing this, I calmly approached him, bent down, and whispered in his ear: *'And there is no Santa Claus.'*

"No Way" he yelled.

'*Way!*' I retorted. I then smiled, assured him that St. Nick was indeed real and watching, gave him a hug, and five minutes later I walked him back to his cottage."

Sean McMannon (Overnight Counselor)

"I like to tell the kids at breakfast that they were all talking in their sleep the night before. They find this hard to believe, but want to know what each was saying.

"So I tell them, 'Guys, all night long I heard the same darn thing: Sean is a *great* guy. Sean is a *great* guy...'

"They love it."

Kay Stolpman (Therapist)

"An eight-year-old boy, Scott, entered our program and was having a hard time adjusting to the place. During school, he got mad about something and refused to leave the computer he was using. Four adults were summoned to deal with him, but none of them could get him to budge or even talk. Finally, I was called. After sizing up the situation, I asked all of the adults to leave and pulled a chair up beside him.

"'You seem kind of upset. Who can blame you? It's not easy being here,' I said. He ignored me.

"'Computers are fun. I can understand why you'd prefer to stay where you are. You haven't had a whole lot of fun lately.' He continued to ignore me.

"I figured it was time to try a new approach. I waited until I got a wee bit of eye contact, and then posed the following question: 'So, you don't speak English, eh?'

"He looked at me with an odd, inquisitive expression. I then began to laugh. Soon, he laughed, as well. He was back in class in two minutes."

Joe Peppin (Teacher extraordinaire – very funny dude)

"I keep a pair of humongous sunglasses in my desk draw. If a kid who has been struggling does well on a quiz or assignment, I meet him at the door the next day wearing the glasses.

"'Why you wearing those glasses?' the kid will ask.

'Because you're getting so *bright* that I need these glasses to protect my eyes. C'mon, look at this. You aced this assignment! Man, I can't handle your brightness! Ow...you're hurtin' me.'

"Sometimes, when the whole class is doing well, I say to them, 'You kids are doing so marvelous today that I feel like yelling it out the window. Excuse me. I think I'm going to do it.' I then go to the window, open it, and yell, 'Hey, everyone, my students are doing m-a-r-v-e-l-o-u-s today. I *love* this class!' Sometimes I let them join me. It's a real hoot – and quite motivating.

"I also keep a Michigan Wolverine cap in my desk – one with a huge 'M' on the front. If I have a day where I'm setting a lot of limits, I often stop the lesson and, in a somewhat animated fashion, proclaim, 'I can't believe what you're making me wear today! You know what I'm talking about.' I then take out the cap and state, 'Yeah, the Meanie cap. And you know, I *hate* wearing the Meanie cap.' Sometimes that's enough to get them back on track.

"I love using props. I think every teacher, heck any person who deals with kids, should make frequent visits to the local joke shop. To reach troubled kids you've got to hook 'em in. And I think humor is the best bait. Plus it's fun."

Wanda Brown (Assistant Unit Director, Adolescent Unit)

"On Thanksgiving we always conduct a funny contest. It's a tradition. Last year we asked all staff members to bring in their high school graduation pictures. We taped them to a poster and had the kids vote for the nerdiest looking high school graduate. It was hysterical. I think it's great when staff allow themselves to be laughed at like that. It helps diffuse the power thing."

Beau Pickles (Special Ed Teacher)

"I was working with a group of younger kids who were swearing too much. One of the boys, Elmo, had a particularly foul mouth and enjoyed ticking off his peers. We (staff and kids) had a meeting to talk about the swearing. We came up with an incentive plan: If the group could go for entire week without uttering as many as twenty swears, the staff would take them out for pizza and ice cream.

"We got to the final day and only thirteen swears had slipped from their lips. The week officially ended at 2:00 p.m. The kids were pretty excited. Halfway through the morning, Elmo swore three times. The other kids were furious. After serving his consequence, Elmo told the group that he was just kidding and wouldn't swear anymore. But an hour later, he deliberately swore three more times. The number of swears stood at nineteen.

"When he returned to the group, Elmo told the kids he was through swearing for the day. Meanwhile Rayshawn, a sometime friend of Elmo's, was getting incredibly anxious. Throughout the day he had pleaded with Elmo not to blow it for them. Two o'clock gradually approached. The second hand was moving excruciatingly slow. Around 1:50 p.m., a mischievous expression popped on Elmo's face. He began to hum to himself.

"Rayshawn's anxiety level was palpable. At 1:54 p.m. he got out of his seat, pointed angrily at Elmo, and warned, 'Elmo, if you fuck this up, I'll kill you!'

I think most kids like me are humor deprived. Man, we haven't had enough laughs in our lives. This is a really important issue. I think a good childcare setting should look as if there isn't a whole lot of structure there, because there's so much fun and goofiness going on. But underneath the fun facade is hang-your-hat-on-it structure. The staff members know exactly what's going on and are cleverly orchestrating the mayhem.

I love being around adults who make me laugh; they're usually upbeat and easygoing. We angry depressos need positive people to pull us out of our ruts. They send us the message that we don't have to take things so seriously. They make life more enjoyable and give us hope. Is there something wrong with that?

Not everyone is naturally funny. But any person can *learn* to be funnier. It doesn't take much – just guts – to buy a joke book and try a few out, to wear a funny hat, to yell out a window, to make a difference.

How about this one: A man goes to the doctor and says, "I've got a problem, Doc. Sometimes I think I'm a teepee and sometimes I think I'm a wigwam. Teepee, wigwam, wigwam, teepee. I need help!"

"I know what your problem is," said the doctor. "You're too tents!"

Loosen up and have some fun, dudes. We're kids. Get us going...

7. The Long Goodbye

Three-quarters of this book has been written and I've barely mentioned my pending discharge. I guess that's typical. No one likes talking about leaving. I think the subject is too loaded for most folks. When kids and staff leave this place, too many people – including those leaving – seem to ignore the subject, or gloss it over.

"Hey, man, let's keep in touch."
"I'll come back and see you guys."
"Let's write to another."

Yada, yada, yada....

When people are getting ready to leave, you hear comments like that all the time. But once a person is really gone you hardly ever hear from them again. Goodbye work is often neglected. That's the sad fact, Jack.

As I wrote earlier, good care for troubled kids involves serious *hello* and *goodbye* work. When a kid leaves a program, the staff really needs to make the termination meaningful; which means dealing with it – not giving it lip service. A proper hello and goodbye sends an important and powerful message to a hurtin' kid: *You matter!*

We've got a staff member named Jody who doesn't duck this issue. She also happens to be my primary counselor. Last week, during dinner, she looked at me and said, "I'm really mad at you, Gus. You had the nerve to get me to like you and now you're taking off.

I think that stinks!" I didn't know what to say. She then looked at Bob Johnson, her jock co-worker, and said, "Bob, aren't you mad at Gus? Doesn't it tick you off when someone you like a whole lot leaves you? I mean, it doesn't seem fair!"

Bob almost choked on his spaghetti. He turned a deep shade of red and spit out the following words: "Yeah, yeah...I ah, I, I'm mad, too." She made ol' Bob move outside his comfort zone.

Jody has been compiling a goodbye scrapbook for me. She's been getting all of the kids and staff to write farewell messages to yours truly. She's also been taking a lot of pictures of my closest friends and me (staff and kids). They all go in the book.

During a kid's last week, the program conducts a goodbye circle for him. All the cottage kids and staff members – including therapists, administrators; anybody who was close to the kid, sit in a circle and say goodbye to him. Many do so by reminiscing about experiences they shared together. At some point during the circle, the kid is presented with his goodbye scrapbook.

I bet ten years from now I'll be dusting off that scrapbook to remember what this place was about, and to reconnect with the people who loved me and turned my life around. Hell, I'll probably be taking out that damn book ten minutes after I'm discharged. Man, I've been here almost four years. In the world of residential care, I'm a dinosaur. They don't keep kids in places like this very long anymore. (They should, if a kid still needs to be here.)

Hey, reader. What if you were fourteen years old again and were told that you *had* to move away from your family...for good? No ifs, ands, or buts...you're leaving. You might be able to see them now and then – but there's no guarantee. Do you think you'd ignore the goodbye process? Do you think you'd make comments like, "Look, I'll call you. We'll get together now and then." Nope. You'd spend a lot of time saying goodbye and processing the numerous emotions your leaving would elicit. You'd deal. Period.

I'm excited and scared about going home. I don't know a lot of kids where my mom lives. I've visited the school I'll be attending; it's big and cold.

Our apartment is pretty small. The landlord, Frank, is a real prick. Our heating system needs serious repair but the jerk doesn't want to fork over the dough to get it fixed. He's also bad at returning phone calls. Last weekend, he cornered me in the landing:

Frank: Hey, kid.
Gus: What?
Frank: You live in some kind of place for bad kids?
Gus: It's none of your business.
Frank: Hey, if you're gonna live here, it is my business, wise-guy.
Gus: You should worry more about our heating system than me. We're thinking of filing a complaint against you.
Frank: Look, I want no problems from you. Don't go bringing me trouble. Keep your pals away from the property. You fuck with me and I'll boot you and your old lady out. Got it?

133

I wanted to get in his face and tell the sucker what I really felt about him, but I *have* learned a few things at the Hills. Instead of letting my impulses take over, I quietly counted; *one, two, three* in my head, and then thought about the shit my mother would go through if he did decide to evict us, and I just walked away. I couldn't believe I stayed so cool. Damn, I think I finally got me some self-control. Yippe-yi-ki-yea! I, the Guster, can self-manage. Wait till they hear about this back at the center. If this had happened three years ago, I probably would have spit in the jerk's face.

One of our neighbors, Barbara, works at a pre-school; she's been real nice to me. Her only child, Jason, is in college. He got a scholarship to M.I.T. A couple of weeks ago, I was sitting on the apartment steps feeling pretty alone, when she appeared with a chess board. We played for hours. While we played, she filled me in more about the town, places to have fun, clubs; man, there's a lot out there.

Moving back with my mother will be easier because of Barbara. I guess it's just like at the center: All it takes is one or two really caring people to get you through. I think every kid who goes home should have a Barbara or two waiting for them. Someone, in addition to your mom and/or dad, who sits with you and helps navigate the new course.

In addition to Barbara, Highland Hills will also make the journey home easier. Pittsiotti, the Executive Director, built it into the rate that when a kid is discharged, people from the program visit him/her regularly for six months. My primary counselor, Jody, and my therapist, Ellen, will each see me once a month for six months. That's pretty cool.

It's mighty overwhelming going home for good when you've lived in a program for such a long time. One day you're living in an intensely structured environment, the next your making decisions you never were allowed to, like: when to eat, what to do, what to wear (I mean really wear), what colors your hair should be, where to place those earrings, what to watch on TV, when to go to bed, who to hang out with. Man, it's great having this new power, but – deep down inside – there's this little voice that keeps asking, *"Can you handle this? Are you ready, man?"* Although dudes like me may talk a tough game, we worry more than we let on.

My mother is working very closely with Highland Hills to make my return home successful. She has spent a lot of time at our program, hanging out in my cottage watching and interacting with the child care staff. Our new family friendly approach has benefited her (and me) tremendously. She's using a lot of what she has learned at the center in our home. So, there is some structure.

Bottom line: When you've lived at a program for a long time, it can take a while before you feel comfortable being home. At times, I feel very out of place. During some visits, I count the minutes till it's time to go back, because that's what's familiar, that's what's safe. But don't get me wrong: I want my freedom. Heck, there are also times when my mother has to drag me kickin' and screamin' back to the center.

Friends, I don't want to live in a group setting anymore. I want what most other kids in this world have: The chance to live life and explore what's out there. I'm ready now. I know this. I've done the work.

But I am scared.

I'm also quite desperate to make friends. At times, I feel painfully alone. Other than Hector, I haven't had too many friends in my life. I hate to admit it, but I'm not that confident about my ability to make and sustain friendships. When I hook up with a kid I like – who I think likes me – I'm always afraid he or she is going to dump me. I often go out of my way to impress the dude – so he or she will like me. Looking back, I've made a real ass of myself on more than one occasion. Sometimes I do things I know are wrong just to be accepted. It's really hard not to. I talked about this friendship stuff in the first book. Man, I'm so used to taking care of number one that I haven't had the time or energy to work on being civil to number 2, 3, 4...and so on; in other words, *friends.*

At the Hills they did a lot of social skills training and put some of us in duos (i.e. matched us with another kid and then had us get together on a weekly basis to *play, talk, and understand* what it meant to be buddies). I loved those duos.

Now it's show time: I got to use what I learned. It feels goods that my mother and so many of the Hills' staff think I'm ready.

"You da man," Jody yells every time I display a shadow of self-doubt.

"Have you made progress here?" she asks.

"Yeah," I answer.

"Have you made some friends?"

"Yeah," I reply

"Well, what does that say?"

"It says Gussy boy can make it. Says I am indeed

Da Man!"

"Slap me five, brother!" she shouts. And our hands meet victoriously.

During my last home visit, I met a kid-

(There's a knock on Gus's door)

"Gus?"
"Yes."

(It's Jody.)

"You have an urgent phone call from Carmelita Escavez."

"It's Hector!" I scream. "He's out of his coma!"

(Gus rushes to the phone.)

"Hello, Mrs. Escavez."
"Gus is that you?"
"Yes. How is Hector? Did he-"
"Hector died this morning. He never awoke from his coma (sobs at the other end of the line)...I guess my boy is finally at peace. No one can hurt him any more."
"NO! NO! NO! He can't be dead. Something's wrong!"

(Gus slams the phone back on the receiver. He's stunned. He can't believe it. Hector... dead?)

"THAT WASN'T THE DEAL!"
"Appelstein...APPELSTEIN...get the hell over here!

Now!"

Appelstein:	What's up?
Gus:	You killed Hector, again. You sono-fabitch! Why? I loved him. I am so pissed.
Appelstein:	You should be. I set you up. I should never have brought him back to life.
Gus:	But you did.
Appelstein:	And I'm sorry about that.

(Long pause)

Gus:	You should be, you friggin' low-life.
Appelstein:	*(surprised)* What are you talkin' about?
Gus:	You didn't have enough balls to let Hector stay dead and that pisses me off. You were right the first time. People need to feel what us kids experience. They need to know what prejudice – in whatever form it takes – can do to us.

Killing Hector made a statement. It hit deep. You shouldn't have given in to me.

I think there's enough hope woven into this book to avoid cheap tricks. |
| Appelstein: | You're right. |

(Long pause)

Gus:	I really did love Hector. I feel bad

138

	that he couldn't tell me he was gay. I should have been a better friend.
Appelstein:	Don't beat yourself up. It was a tough issue. If he had confided in you, I think, in time, you would have been there for him.
Gus:	Why can't people handle differences in others?
Appelstein:	I'm not sure. I guess most of us spend a lot of time worrying about what we think we know. When faced with something or someone different, it might be too much to deal with – so we reject it or the person(s).
Gus:	That's nuts.
Appelstein:	That's life.

(Long pause)

Gus:	We can do better.

(Another knock on the door)

"Gus?"

(It's Jody again.)

"Your mother's here. She heard about Hector. Should I bring her in?"

"Yeah."

"Hi, Gus."

"Hi, Mom...watch out for Appelstein."

(looking around) "Who?"

"Forget it."

"I'm sorry about Hector. I know how much he meant to you."

"I don't want to talk much, Ma. I'm not feeling too good."

"Let's go for a ride."

"No, I'd rather hang out here."

"Gus, I REALLY want you to come with me."

My mother had a very determined look in her face – one I'm not accustomed to seeing.

"Okay," I muttered. "Let's go."

8. Reflections On a Trip Down Lack-of-Memory Lane

My mother and I drove for 40 minutes without saying a word. I thought she was driving us home, but when we arrived at the interstate, she went west instead of east—a curious turn of events.

"Where are we going?" I asked

"You'll find out."

(A few minutes later)

Mom: Your father, Fritz Studelmeyer, was an amazing guy. I fell in love the first time I laid eyes on him. As I wrote in my letter to you, we met at a drug clinic. We were both addicted to heroin. Although he suffered on and off with depression, he still had a wonderful sense of humor, and boy, was he bright. Smartest man I'd ever met. Your poor dad had a miserable childhood. His father, Tom, was a traveling salesman who found family life annoying. Fritz said he had a babe in every port. His mom, Loretta, was one of those stand-by-your-man type wives who never stood up to the bastard. She eventually turned to booze to dull his indifference. I haven't seen her in many years.

Two weeks after leaving the clinic together, we were married. The local Justice of the Peace did the honors. Four months later I was pregnant with you. As stated in my letter, you weren't planned – but after the shock wore off we were both pretty excited. Fritz said he'd be a better dad than his father.

I remember when he called his folks and broke the news about my pregnancy. His mother was ecstatic. His father told him that a kid costs a lot of money – that *he* should know – and not to expect any handouts from him. While speaking to his mother, Fritz heard his father remark "Just what we need, Loretta, another fuckin' druggie!"

After hanging up the phone, your dad put his head down on the kitchen table and cried. He stayed motionless for three hours, until I gently guided him to bed.

Your dad had many interests. I think you'll find this interesting: He loved to write, just like you. He wrote short stories. They were full of intriguing characters, complex plot twists, and breathtaking imagery. He could bring you places with his mind that no other mode of transportation could light a candle to. I loved reading those stories. I pleaded with him to try and get some of them published. He never would. I think he didn't want to be rejected. He'd had enough of that.

I was mesmerized by my mother's words. I was in a state of suspended animation. It was as if my life had stopped and pieces of me that had been missing my entire life were being filled in. I wanted to comment on things she was saying, but all I could do was sit and listen.

Mom: Shortly after his suicide, I threw all his stories away. I was out of my mind, I was so mad at him. I tried to obliterate his memory. His death hurt me something awful. I didn't see it coming.
That's why I never talked about him with you. Out of sight, out of mind. I know now that was wrong – for you, and for me. I'm sorry.

Gus: What did he look like?

(Gus's mother chuckled to herself.)

Mom: Why you, of course. He was a big husky guy with long red hair, freckles, and a smile that could light up a room. He usually tied his hair in a ponytail. I think what did it for me was his eyes. Like yours, they were brown – and there was something magnetic about them. Those beautiful suckers had a way of pulling me close.
He liked to wear hiking boots. He said they made him feel like a man. During the summer, he'd wear sandals occasionally, but he loved those boots.

Gus: Was he always into drugs?

Mom: No. That's the sad thing. Given his past,

he had led a pretty straight life up until the year before we met. At that time, he took in a roommate who hid a serious drug habit. Shortly thereafter your dad got laid off from a job he loved, broke up with a girlfriend he had been seeing for two years, and had a couple of serious run-ins with his dad over money...and the rest is history. He started doing drugs to *'numb the pain.'* He told me it was the worst thing he could have done. Two months later he was addicted to heroin. It was tragic and he knew it.

I was the classic bad-girl during my teen years. I lashed out in reaction to the abuse I had suffered and I didn't care much about myself. I felt like a piece of crap. Your dad actually helped ground me. He made me feel special. I guess that's why it hurt so damn much when he was no longer there.

When some one believes in you, there ain't nothing you can't do. The five or six months we spent together were one of the best periods of my life.

Gus: Why did he off himself?

(Long pause. Gus's mother struggles to fight back the tears.)

Mom: I guess it was a combination of things. He stopped taking his antidepressant medication two weeks before; he said it was making him tired. His father kept throwing in the occasional dig. And being off the heroin was a new experience for him. He lost his crutch. Frankly, I think it was self-doubt that did him in. I believe your poor dad just didn't have enough confidence that he could cut it any longer. He didn't leave a note. That pissed me off, too. I wish he had at least said goodbye...

(Tears flow steadily from her eyes. Neither one talks for a while.)

Gus: So where are we going?

Mom: We're going to visit Loretta.

Gus: What?

Mom: We're going to see your dad's mom. I haven't seen her in fourteen years. I looked her up on the Internet. I called her last week. We spoke for two hours. I think she's changed a whole lot – for the better.

Gus: What about Tom?

Mom: She divorced the jerk one year after Fritz died. She hasn't seen him or a bottle of booze in ten years.

Gus: How does she feel about us coming?

Mom: She said she's been waiting fourteen years for us to call.

The car drifted along the powerful interstate. Trucks from at least seven states passed us by. Nondescript cars and SUVs dotted both sides of the median. I tried to look at the faces of the drivers. I wondered if any one of them was going somewhere as important as I was. I didn't think so.

Mom: There's route 290 East. We take that for about five miles to exit 12. Her house is one mile up on the right. It's white with blue shutters, number 80. Are you ready for this?

Gus: Are you?

Mom: Let's do it.

Twelve minutes later, our tired pick-up truck rolled over the reddish gravel of the driveway at 80 Troy Street. The two hearts in the vehicle were thumpin' big-time. We slowly made our way to the front door. Prior to knocking [there was a sign that read - Please knock, bell broken] we looked at each other and without words affirmed our reason for being there. As I went to knock, the door suddenly flung open.

Loretta: You must be Gus...

Smiling broadly and wearing an old flowered apron, Loretta looked like the warm, doting grand-mother I had so hoped to see. On pure impulse, I took two steps forward and gave her a monster hug. The old coot gave it right back to me. Man, it was total bliss. I felt like I was connecting with a part of me that had been lost for a long time. Afterwards, my mother repeated the exchange, and when we had all dried our tears, we ate chocolate chip cookies and talked.

It was a somewhat sad but glorious get-together. Grandma Loretta had placed all her photo albums on the dining room table. I saw my dad from infancy to manhood. My fingers needed to touch every picture. At times, I'd pick up a photo of Dad looking straight at the camera, and would feel as if he was truly looking at me. Ain't that kind of weird? I think his spirit entered mine that afternoon. I never felt more whole.

Dad's death was a tragic wake-up call to Grandma Loretta. After mourning her only child's death, she began to stand up to her husband. He wouldn't change, so she booted "the two-timing, insensitive dirt bag" out of the house. At some point, I'm going to track him down. I'd like to try and understand why he opted to make so many bad choices in his life. I've learned to be quite careful about judging people. Heck, kids like me get judged poorly all the time – and we're not bad. We just need people to reach out to us, and not give up when their hands get slapped. Maybe there's more to Grandpa then what I've been told. Maybe he needs a hand. My hand.

Halfway through the visit, Grandma suggested we go for a walk. She lived in a modest neighborhood. Most of the houses were small but well cared for. Ten minutes into the walk, we found ourselves in front of the Kenmore Cemetery.

"Your dad is buried here. Would you like to visit his grave site?" I was stunned. I had not anticipated this. I think I forgot to breathe.

"Yes," I choked out. "I'd like that very much."

Grandma Loretta visited her son's plot every week. It was on her way to work. She was employed as a bookkeeper at a family owned tire business in town. M & L Tires was the last family owned business in her area. She liked being at a place where a family struggled, laughed, and worked together.

"This is it, Gus."

Dad's site was adorned with beautiful flowers and was obviously well cared for. Good old Loretta.

I faced my father...

At first, all I could do was look and ponder the moment. My whole body trembled. Finally, I started talking. It was hard. I had to pause a lot. I felt a bit weak-kneed...

"Dad. It's your son, Gus. How's it going? I saw some of your pictures today. I liked the ponytail. You and me look a lot alike. Ain't that something?

"I'm sorry you were so unhappy. Wish I could have done something about that.

"Hey, Mom and I are finally back together. It's feeling okay. She's here with me now. Doesn't she look good?

"Look, I want you to know I'm pissed as hell that you killed yourself. That was really dumb, man. We never got to meet. What the hell were you thinking? But don't worry, I'll never do what you did. It may sound corny, but you got to face things in life. (*Tears well in Gus's eyes, and he lowers his head.*)

"I think we gotta go now. We'll be back.

"I'm real glad we finally met. It means so much to me to know I'm your son. I love you, Dad."

I bent down and picked up some dirt from the

base of his tombstone. I placed it in my pocket. We quietly walked back to the house. After I was convinced that we had heard every story that Grandma Loretta could remember about Dad, we said goodbye.

Oh, yeah, we'll be back.

9. Keyon's Story

The experience of meeting Loretta and seeing Dad was truly amazing. I had so many thoughts and emotions flowing through my brain following that visit. Sadness, anger, exhilaration, guilt, remorse, joy...they all partied in my head. Connecting with long lost Dad kind of filled me in. That black hole in me, the one named Fritz, is a lot smaller now; yet even though I feel better on the inside, on the outside I'm struggling.

I don't feel like moving forward. I just want to suspend my existence for a while, so that I can savor and work through this momentous experience. Man, this "dad" thing is big, and I simply don't have the energy or desire to focus on anything else right now. I don't think people realize how much it takes out of us to do the "psychological" work. Dudes, it can bring you to your knees.

"Appelstein."

"APPELSTEIN!"

"What?"

"Take over."

"What?"

"You heard me. I said take over."

"What do you mean?"

"I mean, I'm taking a break from this book and everything else in life. I'm gonna find me a reclining chair - one with big, leather cushions. I'm then gonna sit down, clasp my hands behind my head, kick my feet up, close my eyes, and think about where I've been and where I'm going. I may even do a little dreaming about me and Dad on a fishin' trip, canoeing down a lazy river on a crisp autumn morning, looking for that big mouthed bass that got away. So Chuckeroo, you're on your own for a chapter. Can you handle it?"

Appelstein:	What should I write about it?
Gus:	Look, knucklehead, do I have to do everything for you?
Appelstein:	C'mon, give me a suggestion before you take your chill out.
Gus:	Fine. Write something inspirational. Give hope to the readers and to me. We could use some at this point. Of course, you know what I'm talking about.
Appelstein:	Yeah, I think I do. Hey, make sure you come back.
Gus:	Don't worry, Jack. We've got some unfinished business with Jay. Tootaloo, dude...

I still find it amazing that kids like Gus can endure so much and still make something of their lives. I guess it's true that most kids are incredibly resilient. (Thank the Lord for bestowing this attribute.)

Oftentimes, folks who work with troubled kids don't see the end result, never hear the success stories. Sometimes, we just get lost in the daily grind.

Every now and then I wonder if it's all worth it. All the hard work, the sacrifices, the crazy hours. At times, even I wonder whether us social service types make enough of a difference. I can get discouraged with the best of them.

Fortunately, my moments of doubt are short-lived.

Because *I know* we make a difference. *I know* every positive interaction with a troubled kid is significant. *I know* that I don't have to see a kid ten years from now (doing well) *to know* that what we did mattered. I've learned this lesson...because I've had some great teachers.

During the past twenty-five years, I've met a number of remarkable kids. Each one has left his or her imprint on my soul and enriched my life. When I get discouraged about work and start to doubt my (our) efforts, I often think about one kid in particular: Keyon. He has been, and will always be, a remarkable teacher. Gus suggested I write something inspirational...let me tell you about my buddy Keyon.

For six years I was the Program Director and Treatment Coordinator of a mid-sized residential setting. I loved my job. And then one day, it didn't feel right anymore so I quit. To put bread on the table (I had just gotten married and my wife was worried about our survival), I signed on with a social service temp agency, while I slowly developed my training and consultation business.

It was a strange existence. One day I'm making a decent salary and overseeing a staff of 40 professionals, the next I'm driving 90 minutes to do an awake overnight at a downtrodden group home for negligible pay. I told my worried wife to have faith: "Good things happen to good people." I thought that sounded better than, "Guess you married a loser, honey."

After a couple months of awake overnights, the temp agency called and informed me that a foster care agency had a temporary opening for a Masters level caseworker. Hallelujah! I can sleep once more! The agency was small and didn't have a lot of resources, but that never stopped them from trying to do it right. I had great respect for the executive director and program director. I still do.

One month into the job, I was asked to visit a young boy, age nine, who was struggling in his foster placement. He was stealing food from the kitchen, lying a lot, "manipulating," and not doing well in school. His current foster family had intended to adopt him, but was now having second thoughts. I was sent in to help out.

Keyon, age nine, was a scrawny little African American kid with an engaging smile and handsome features. During our first visit, we ate lunch at Papa Gino's. Keyon told me he liked anchovies on his pizza. But we settled on less radical toppings. Over lunch, Keyon raved about his foster family. He could not have been more positive. Months later, we learned that some bad things were happening in the home. Keyon's foster parents took in too many kids and the stress got to them. Mistakes were made. Good people sometimes do less-than-good things.

Years later, Keyon told me that he lied about them because he was afraid we'd put him with a new family that would treat him even worse. *A bird in the hand is worth two in the bush.*

Keyon had never known a safe and nurturing home. Prior to entering foster care, he had been physically abused in every setting in which he had lived. He never knew his father and his mom was unable to overcome her drug problems. Some of the bad things that happened to Keyon were quite severe. He was locked in closets, burned with cigarette butts, and forced to eat his own vomit. Yet, through it all, he never gave up on himself. Keyon had spunk. He was fiercely proud, and was a fighter (in the best sense of the word).

I started seeing him every week. I enjoyed our visits. He had a good sense of humor and was a decent little athlete. I remember the first time we threw a football together. Although he could barley grip it, he threw the leather off that sucker. I kept moving back, but he'd still manage to throw it over my head.

Because of the problems at his foster home, it wasn't long before we had to find Keyon a new family. Eileen, his caseworker, found an inner city family with a large house and plenty of heart. If there was a Hall of Fame for caseworkers, Eileen would get my vote. Sweet, kind, and incredibly thorough, Eileen worked tirelessly on Keyon's behalf.

Keyon's new foster mother, Rosa, was warm and nurturing, but she had her tough side, as well. For the first time in my little buddy's life, he had a maternal figure that treated him the way a mother should. It wasn't easy for him to handle. On the one hand, he loved it; he'd melt in her presence. On the other hand, he was deathly afraid that she'd abandon him like everyone else had, so he acted out to push her away – to stop her from getting too close.

One morning, he just broke down and tearfully recounted to Rosa all the episodes of physical abuse he had suffered. On and on he went. It was terribly sad. I remember visiting him that afternoon. Rosa was still visibly upset. She loved the kid and it broke her heart that he had suffered such atrocities. I told Rosa that it was her love and nurturing that got Keyon to open up.

For the first time in his life, I think he felt comfortable in a home setting, which gave him the courage to bare his soul. I also told her that his behavior might get worse now that his past was out in the open and he would be consciously dealing with it.

Sadly, I was right. Keyon's behavior regressed significantly. I think he went back and tried to get what he had missed in his early years. His behavior often resembled that of a two-year-old. Defiance, poops down the heating duct, lying, tantrums...he let them have it.

I did my best to sit with Rosa and explain why Keyon's regression, from a developmental and psychological perspective, was actually a good thing. Sometimes I succeeded, sometimes I didn't. During this period, she routinely threatened to get rid of him. I couldn't blame her; his behavior was extreme. I remember one day spending four straight hours on the phone with her (during my only vacation that year), pleading with her not to reject him. She finally relented.

Eventually, his behavior grew so problematic that he needed to be placed in an intensive, short-term, diagnostic residential setting. When he entered the program, the plan was for him to be stabilized and then returned to Rosa and her family; they weren't going to give up on him. In fact, she and her husband were considering adoption.

The new setting was hard on Keyon. He hated being separated from Rosa's warmth and love. A few weeks into this new placement, a bomb dropped on

Keyon's case. Because Rosa's husband had a minor legal problem in his past, Keyon would not be allowed to return to their family. The state had instituted new guidelines for foster parents.

Eileen and I were devastated. We thought the news might break Keyon. It seemed so unfair. *How much could this kid take?*

I remember the day we told him that he wouldn't be allowed to return to his foster family. Eileen couldn't stop crying. She really loved that kid. I told Keyon that I had never met a kid who had experienced so much bad luck in his life, and that at some point it just had to change, and that both Eileen and I would be with him until that happened. Upon hearing the news, he could barely speak. The little guy was gutted. It was one of the saddest days of my life.

In the following days, his behavior grew progressively worse and he was eventually placed in a residential treatment center. Around this time, I quit the foster care agency, but continued to see Keyon in a kind of "Big Brother" capacity. I certainly wasn't going to quit on him. Like Eileen, I loved the kid. I told him we'd be "brothers for life." And I meant it.

For the next year or so, Keyon did relatively well at the residential program. I continued to see him on a regular basis. We always had a lot of fun together (still do). We saw a lot of movies, ate a lot of Whoppers and seafood, frequented the local arcade on numerous occasions, built model airplanes, and threw the football around.

I remember one time treating Keyon to three humongous lobsters, plus a full plate of steamers. I almost choked when it came time to pay the check.

Afterwards, we went for ice cream. I asked Keyon whether he wanted two scoops or three on his cone. He looked back at me and said "Charlie, I'd like three, but I want to save you some money." Five years later, we're still laughing about that line.

Keyon was always a good listener. I think he liked when I'd normalize a situation for him. In other words, explain why kids who have been through hell, might act in a certain way. But in the early days he wasn't too thrilled about taking responsibility for his actions. His defensiveness was quite understandable. Who else took care of Keyon, but Keyon? The world had never been a safe place.

Kids who have been repeatedly put down and hurt often avoid things that can cause pain or embarrassment. Can you blame them? But not Keyon. School wasn't an easy place for him. Because of the turmoil in his early life, the kid entered third grade unable to read. To this day, Keyon says this fact - his inability to read in 3rd grade – was worse than any of the abuse he incurred.

"I can and have worked through the abuse. I still have to learn," he recently told me. Despite his educational shortcomings, Keyon *never* shied away from learning.

Deep inside of my pal burns an incredible desire to be the best he can be. For some inexplicable reason, I sense Keyon has always believed in himself, and has known that he is special and can ascend to great heights. This doesn't mean he possesses glowing self-esteem; he has really struggled in this area. But in his soul, the kid knows he is a warrior destined to win any battle.

Back to the story...

I kept in touch with Eileen. She was working hard to find Keyon a new family. One day she called me and was incredibly excited. One of the child care workers at Keyon's program, Rhonda Roberts, had suggested to her parents, Barbara and Jim, that they consider adopting Keyon.

To make a long story short, this is exactly what happened. For the first time in my young friend's life, lady luck paid him a visit. I think the Roberts were sent from heaven. A warm and wonderful African American family, they had raised three great kids – who were now adults – and were committed to giving one more kid the chance to grow up under their roof.

Keyon transitioned very well into the Roberts' household. I think the first time I visited Keyon at the Roberts', I just wanted to cry. You could not have asked for a better situation. The Roberts lived in a nice suburb, in a nice home, with a nice backyard, with nice neighbors, and they were good people.

Frankly, I was a little nervous at first that they wouldn't want me to stay involved with Keyon. Barbara quickly allayed this fear. She and her husband welcomed me with open arms. We've been good friends ever since.

A year or so later, Keyon was officially adopted by the Roberts. On all fronts he continued to make outstanding progress. Right from the get-go, Barbara signed him up for Pop Warner football. Although he was still a wee bit on the scrawny side, he loved the game and was strong as an ox. (She also religiously stayed on top of his studies.)

Right away, it became apparent that Keyon and football were a pretty good match. At the end of his first season, three kids from the town had been hospitalized after being tackled by Keyon. He could run like the wind and hit with the force of freight train.

Two years later Keyon and his family faced a BIG decision: Where would he attend High School? His accomplishments in Pop Warner had not gone unnoticed, and the football coach at the public high school in Keyon's town was salivating in expectation of Keyon joining his team.

Keyon had become a standout in Pop Warner. He played both sides of the ball. On offense, he was an elusive yet slashing running back; on defense, a bone-crushing linebacker. And he still wasn't that big. For the previous two years, Keyon attended a school for kids with learning disabilities. He made significant academic progress. It was important to him. It was decision time.

Keyon did not want to go to his local high school. He wanted to play Division One football (the highest level) for a top team in the state, at a school with extremely rigorous academic standards. Frankly, I thought he was nuts.

I worried that he was too small to compete at the Division One level, and I was sure the academics would overwhelm him. I was afraid for him. He wasn't. *Damn, where does the kid get it from?* I'd think to myself.

He was accepted at the Division One school and did great his first year, as a sophomore. Sure, he needed extra tutoring and help on the home front to pass all his classes, but he did.

During the previous summer, he had a nice growth spurt and entered the football season at five feet, nine inches tall, weighing 160 pounds: Still not very big for Division One football. Yet, Mr. Tenacity, good ol' Keyon, won the starting outside linebacker position and played every game. I don't think he hospitalized any of his opponents, but he had some memorable plays during the year.

Folks, Keyon was born to carry a football. In Pop Warner he made runs that took your breath away. During his sophomore season, Keyon was too shy to tell his coach that he wanted to be a running back in addition to his current linebacking duties. Making matters worse, a fellow sophomore, L.B., joined the squad, along with Keyon, and was an exceptional runner.

Early in their sophomore seasons, I watched L.B. carry the ball and muttered to myself *"Damn! That kid's a great running back. Keyon will never get a chance as long as L.B.'s on the team."* I felt awful. I knew how much Keyon wanted to carry the ball; but it didn't look good. Never, I repeat *never*, underestimate this kid.

Keyon reported for his first football practice of his junior year standing 5' 11" tall and weighing 190 pounds of rock-hard muscle. He had lifted weights every day since the previous season had ended. Still a bit shy, Keyon caught a break when other members of the team let the head coach know that he wanted a shot at running back.

It was a cool, crisp, Monday afternoon. During practice the coach pulled Keyon aside.

Coach: I hear you want to run the ball?

Keyon: Yeah.

Coach: Can you run?

Keyon: Yeah,

Coach: Why didn't you tell me this before?

Keyon: *(looking down)* I don't know.

Coach: Here's the deal. We have one more pre-season game on Saturday. I'll let you practice with the offense this week. During the game, I'll give you three plays. If you don't show something, we'll end this experiment. Okay?

Keyon: Okay.

On Saturday, the first quarter was unremarkable. L.B. was not gaining much yardage and the team appeared somewhat sluggish. On defense, Keyon was pounding his opponents...and waiting.

Mid-way through the second quarter, Keyon's team had the ball. Keyon was standing on the sideline watching. In his mind, in his soul, he knew he had been *watching* for long enough. Suddenly, the coach appeared before him.

"Keyon, remember the deal. You've got three plays to show me something. Go on in..."

In the stands, Barbara, Jim, and Rhonda Roberts grabbed each other's hands and tried to calm their hearts. Onto to the field trotted Keyon Roberts. My friend. A kid who had lived through hell but had never quit.

He entered the huddle and the quarterback called the play. The plan was for Keyon to run through a hole in the middle of the line. It was the same play that had been called for L.B. a few times earlier in the game. On each occasion, L.B. had been stopped for little gain. Now it was Keyon's turn. His team was 56 yards from the opposing team's end zone.

"Hut! Hut! Hut!"

The ball was snapped. The quarterback took a step back, pivoted, and handed the ball to Keyon. With eyes focused on the hole and feet driving, Keyon advanced two yards past the line of scrimmage before being mauled by two huge defensive linemen. In the stands it looked like he was going down. But his feet never stopped moving, his heart never stopped pumping, and he broke the tackle of the two behemoths and darted to the right. Immediately, a swarm of linebackers moved in. Keyon stopped. I mean, he literally stopped, and the poor suckers ran right by him. Changing direction to the left, an opposing cornerback was his next obstacle. At the precise moment the two made contact, Keyon spun around with amazing speed and left the dude in his dust. The only thing left now separating Keyon from the end zone was one lone cornerback. Keyon raced to the goal line. The opposing cornerback was gaining on him from the right. Just as he was about to make the tackle, Keyon slowed and cut dramatically to the right. The cornerback grasped for Keyon's jersey, but it was too late.

In the stands, tears welled in the eyes of the Roberts, as they pumped their hands, stomped their feet, and raised their fists in triumph. On the sideline, Keyon's coach was excited and *stunned*. Coaches can live a lifetime without ever witnessing such an extraordinary play. Keyon's coach is a real good man. He didn't know what he had in Keyon. I'm glad they are together.

Two steps in front of Keyon lay the goal line. No one was going to catch him. Behind him lay a pile of bruised bodies...and a mountain of abuse. On the field and in life, he just can't be stopped.

As he crossed the goal line, a young mother in southern New Hampshire was changing her baby's diaper and trying to do five things at once. She was tired, and looked a bit gaunt. She didn't hear any cheers that day. After all, people don't cheer wildly for a good diaper change. What Eileen heard and saw that day were the precious actions of her kid. *But she was there – at the game - and Keyon knew it.*

Although the folks in the stands could only see uniform-clad players celebrating wildly in the end zone, at the far end was a small, invisible group of fans slapping each other five, dancing,' and huggin'. Me, Eileen, Rosa, and the Roberts; we were all there having a ball. Poor Keyon can't get rid of us. Wherever he goes – we're with him. And I'm telling you, that end zone felt great!

Keyon wants to play pro football. I ain't doubtin' him. Are you?

I think deep inside of all of us is a person who can score touchdowns. Sometimes the obstacles standing in the way to the end zone are huge, but if you keep your feet moving and your eyes focused, if you can draw on the courage that's in your gut, you can get there.

Of course, it doesn't hurt to have some help along

the way.

Hey, the next time you feel hopeless and are considering giving up, why not close your eyes and reach out your hand...grab onto the back of Keyon's jersey and hold on, man – 'cause it going to be one helluva run to daylight.

10. The Brickmans Come to Highland Hills

The Brickmans are coming soon to say goodbye to Jay. They kept their word. They are honoring the process.

I was asked to see the kid. He's not in good shape. Can you blame him? I headed over to his cottage. He was in his bedroom. He didn't want to come out. He let me in.

Jay: I don't want to do this.

Gus: Why would you want to? This is brutal, man.

Jay: I'm not gonna see them.

Gus: Yeah, you are.

Jay: What?

Gus: I said, 'Yes, you are going to visit with them.'

Jay: Fuck you. You can't tell me what to do.

Gus: No, I can't. I can only tell you that if you don't say goodbye, it will bother you forever.

Jay: I don't care.

Gus: Seeing them will suck. It will be hard. But you gotta do it, dude. Believe me, I know.

(moving a few steps closer to Jay, with passion in his voice) I never had the chance, you have today, to say goodbye to the families that kicked me out. I wish I had. I might have felt a little better about myself.

You read the Brickman's letter. You need

	to hear some of the good stuff face-to-face. You gotta hear that they still think you're one heck of a kid. Don't be a jerk; don't blow this opportunity.
Jay:	I ALWAYS SCREW UP EVERYTHING! No family will ever want me. I HATE fuckin' families.
Gus:	Hey, you had some good times with the Brickmans, didn't you?
Jay:	No.
Gus:	Not one good moment?
Jay:	No.
Gus:	C'mon, be real.
Jay:	Maybe a few.
Gus:	There you go.
	If you can have a few, you can have a lot more. Have hope. You're a great kid. You have a lot to offer.
Jay:	No one will ever want me. No one ever has.
Gus:	Hey, that's how I felt when I was your age. But look at me; I'm back with my mother and we're doing okay.
Jay:	My mother's dead, asshole.
Gus:	Oh God, I didn't know. That really sucks.
Jay:	I never knew her. She died when I was born.
Gus:	That's awful. I bet she would have loved you very much.
Jay:	Who cares? People can tell you they love you and then let things happen to you.
Gus:	What does that mean?
Jay:	Nothing.

Gus:	What kind of things?
Jay:	Forget it. Nothing.
Gus:	Jay...

(Jay closes his eyes, covers his ears with his hands, begins rocking his head and humming.)

I thought about Jay's words: "People can tell you they love you and then let things happen to you." Now's not the time to push him – *(is there ever a time?)* – and I ain't no therapist. But I think he's getting ready to talk about stuff. Serious stuff. Like maybe bad people doing bad things to him – probably sexual. Kids like Jay and me don't usually touch someone in their private areas, masturbate all over the place, and talk the gutter way because it's been a wonderful life. Behavior is a message. Always.

Dealing with a difficult loss can trigger painful memories in kids who have been abused and rejected by adults. Loss loosens. Like an onion, a bad loss peels away our defenses, leaving us highly exposed to the outside elements (like adults). A sensitive but sharp staff member can view these periods (when a kid is dealing with an evocative loss) to help a "grieving" kid to work through other painful issues in his past. It's not unusual for a kid to reveal past abuses shortly after a favorite staff member announces that she is leaving.

This meeting with the Brickmans is triggering a lot of crappola in Jay. I'm glad that I'm with him. It's really hard to be alone with the memories. I was just like Jay when I first got here. It took me a long time before I could talk about Ronald, the scumbag who sexually abused me. I held in my feelings about the abuse (but certainly acted them out). Shame, guilt, embarrassment, rage...they consumed me – when I wasn't successful in blocking them out.

When I finally started talking to Ellen about Ronald, she was wonderful; let me know, right from the start, that the abuse wasn't my fault, and that she wouldn't think any less of me if I told her about it. I had been afraid that she'd think I was a fag or something if I described what Ronald did to me. I'll never forget what she told me: "You're a great kid, Gus. If you have the courage to talk about the sexual abuse, you'll be a hero. Heroes run into burning houses and pull people out. They take a lot of risk, but save lives. If you talk about this, you'll be running into the flames of your personal hell, but you might just save the life of a kid I think is pretty special."

She blew me away. At bedtime, I muffled my tears by clutching a pillow to my face. For the first time in my whole life, I went to bed feeling okay about myself. I couldn't help but cry.

I'm glad Jay is here. Residential treatment has helped me; it will help him. I hope they let him stay here long enough to do the work. Times are different now.

He seemed to be calming down. It was time for a different approach. I sat down by his side.

Gus: Hey, buddy, can I read you a story?

Jay: What?

Gus: It's a true story about a kid who went through everything you're going through

	– but he ended up happy, with a family that loved him.
Jay:	Yeah, right.
Gus:	I'm not bullshitting you. He had a terrible life for a lot of years.
Jay:	Did he get sent to a shit-hole place like this?
Gus:	Yeah, for a few years.
Jay:	Did he get restrained?
Gus:	A few times.
Jay:	Did he get kicked out of families?
Gus:	Yeah.
Jay:	What's his name?
Gus:	Keyon.
Jay:	Read it if you want. I don't care.

I read Jay most of Chapter Eight. *He got into it.* Kids like Jay, like me, often benefit from being read stories that we can relate to. (Ellen calls it bibliotherapy.) Sometimes we feel like we're the only ones in the world going through this hell. It's comforting to hear that we're not alone. It's even better to hear that some of us rise up and beat the odds. We "at-risk" kids love learning about sports stars and other famous people who had tough childhoods. It gives us hope, man.

Jay:	Do you think I could ever play basketball like Keyon plays football?
Gus:	Oh, most definitely! I think you can do anything you put your mind to. It just takes hard work.

(Long pause)

C'mon, let's get this over with.

(Gus puts his arm on Jay's shoulder and guides him towards the door.)

Jay: That's PC
Gus: Screw PC!
Jay: I don't want to talk to them.
Gus: You don't have to. Just listen. We can do this. C'mon, brother.

We slowly walked, along with Paul, to the final meeting with the Brickmans. Jay was in the middle. He looked pale and nervous.

It was like a scene out of a death-row movie:

"DEAD MAN WALKIN'!"

"DEAD MAN WALKIN'!"

Me, Mary (Jay's therapist), Carla and Fred Brickman, and Jay were seated in a circle in Mary's office. There was an awkward silence. No one looked comfortable. Jay stared at a spot on the rug below Mary's feet.

Mary: I think we all know why we're here today. This isn't easy for any of us. Jay, you're showing a lot of courage. Carla, Fred, this is Gus Studelmeyer. We told you about him.
Carla: It's nice to finally meet you.

172

Gus: You too.
Fred: Yes, thanks for helping Jay.
Gus: Hey, it's been my pleasure.

Jay continued to avoid eye contact with the Brickmans. He was beginning to squirm in his seat. The poor kid was really hurting.

Mary: Carla, would you like to start.
Carla: Jay, honey, both Fred and I are sorry about how you left us. We don't want you to ever think that you're some bad kid who we wanted to get rid of.

(Carla puts her head down, struggling to the words.)

...We just weren't sure that we could give you what you needed.

Fred: You're a great kid, Jay, one who needs more help than we can give right now.
Let's face it, it got difficult at our house. There were some bad feelings.

(Fred struggles with the next sentence.)

We...we...ah...think this is the right place for you to work on your issues and then, when the time is right *(pause)* meet a new family *(longer pause)* and get a fresh start.
Jay looked miserable. The Brickmans didn't sound too convincing. This meeting was supposed to

help. But something didn't feel right.

Carla: *(tearfully)* But we'll always have a special place in our hearts for you. We have a lot of *wonderful* memories.

Gus: *(standing up)* Excuse me, folks. But something doesn't feel right. My gut is telling me that this meeting is bullshit. *(Whoa, did I just say what I think I said?)*

(Jay looks at Gus with a surprised expression. Mary's face contorts.)

Mary: Gus, maybe-

Gus: I can't sit and listen to this. Let's go, Jay.

(Gus gets up and motions to Jay to come.)

Mary: Fred, Carla, I'm sorry about this. I-

Carla: Gus, why is this bullshit?

Gus: Because it just hit me: I don't think you two want to do this. I think you both still love this kid and should stick by him. Guys, work with Highland Hills to give Jay what he needs, and when he's ready – bring him home, dammit!

Mary: *(Jumping to her feet, approaching Gus in agitation)* Gus, can I see you outside?

Gus: *(Thinking, 'Oh, Shit, what did I do?' and following Mary out of the room)* I'm sorry, but I had to say it.

Mary: *(taking her time, trying to regain her composure)* You made things worse. You set

174

	up Carla and Fred. This isn't going to help Jay. The Brickmans will look even worse in his eyes. Maybe it was not a good idea for you to be in this meeting.
Gus:	Maybe it was.
Mary:	Gus, listen-
Gus:	No, you listen. I don't blame you for being upset. You don't want anyone to get hurt. You know your stuff, but I know these people-
Mary:	What do you mean? How could you know them?
Gus:	Because I visited their house to-
Mary:	You what?
Gus:	I visited them last month. I wanted them to say a proper goodbye to Jay.
Mary:	Did anyone approve the visit?
Gus:	Hell, no. But I'd do it again tomorrow. It was the right thing to do.
Mary:	We'll need to discuss this at a later time. Right now we-
Gus:	*(cutting her off)* Mary, I'm not sure Carla and Fred want to terminate from this kid.
Mary:	Look, we go back *now* and you apologize for putting them on the spot, say something helpful, and I'll do damage control. You got it?
Gus:	No. I don't GOT it. But you're calling the shots. I'll do what you say.

I'm guessing that if you enjoy a good marriage, and you stay together for a while, spoken words are often replaced with familiar looks. Like a code. When

175

Mary and I stepped outside the room, Carla glanced longingly at her husband of eight years and conveyed a message that wasn't too hard for Fred to decipher: *Gus is right.*

(Fred looks deep into his wife's eyes, smiles warmly, and slowly nods his head. Rising gently from her seat, Carla approaches her husband. He rises to meet her.)

Fred: Are you really sure, hon?
Carla: Yeah. Are you?
Fred: Oh God, yes.

(They grasp each other's hands and squeeze hard.)

Four feet away the little guy was confused. The meeting was not going as planned. Somewhere deep in the caverns of Jay's mind, a little voice was telling him that the Brickmans had changed their mind and would again be his family. What the hell is going on?

He had no choice but to ignore these thoughts. Too much risk involved. He sat expressionless. Mary and I returned to the room

Mary: Okay. Gus and I have talked and-
Carla: Excuse me, Mary, but ever since Gus came to our house, we've been rethinking this whole thing. Hearing him today was our ultimate wake-up call. Mary, we're not a family without Jay.
Fred: *(turning to face Jay)* We know you've got

some issues to work out, and that we can be better parents, and that it might be a while before you're ready to live with us again.

(Carla gets up and approaches Jay. On the way over, she uses her sleeve to wipe away a few stray tears.)

Carla: But we love you, pal.

(extending her arms) You're *our* boy.

(Jay rises hesitantly, and then flies to her arms.)

Jay: Mom...

(Fred soon joins them for a long and hearty family hug.)

Mary: *(Whispering)* You're a jerk, Studelmeyer.
Gus: Yeah. I've heard that.
Mary: They've got a lot of work ahead of them. It won't be easy.
Gus: Yeah.
Mary: *(teary-eyed)* Gus, I'm really glad he met you.
Gus: Nah. I'm the lucky one.

I really wish the meeting had gone that well. Sorry reader, I set you up. I was curious whether you'd buy Jay's response to the Brickmans' change of heart. If you did, I've done a lousy job of explaining what makes us kids tick.

Here's what happened:

When Carla approached Jay, he didn't fly into her arms; no, he flew from the room. He dashed across the campus with Mary and me running after him in hot pursuit. Dr.Pittsiotti was just pulling out of the driveway when he almost hit Jay. Thank God for brakes.

Pittsiotti chased him down and put him in a bear hug. Jay was screaming to be let go. We approached and after a half-hour got him to settle down. The poor kid was confused as hell. He didn't know what to make of the meeting. He was preparing to say good-bye and now the Brickmans wanted him back. He felt like a human yo-yo; one that was wrapped way too tight. He wanted desperately to go back to them, but couldn't bear to think that this could all happen again. You're here, you're not, you're here....How's a kid who has been bounced around all his life going to trust anyone when this kind of stuff happens? I guess I shouldn't have said anything. But it just felt right.

Luckily, it all turned out well in the end. I have it on reliable sources that after a series of meetings between the Brickmans and Highland Hills, Jay was reunited with them. The Brickmans know that it could be a while before Jay is ready to live with them. They don't care. He's their boy. Ain't that somethin'?

~

Seven weeks later, Jay returned to the Brickmans for a weekend visit. It felt wonderful to be home. He excitedly entered his bedroom and looked around to

make sure everything was where it should be. Something was different. Out of the corner of his eye he
noticed a foreign object on the shelf over his bed. He
walked over to it, reached up and grabbed—*a football?*
Looking at it closer, he saw that it was signed:

Jay,
See you in the end zone!
Your friend,
Keyon

Jay smiled and tucked the football under his arm.
That day *he* was the hero.

11. Final Thoughts

In a few months I'll be saying goodbye to Jay and Highland Hills. I'll miss my little buddy. I'll miss this place. But I'm ready to go. I've worked my butt off. Coming to grips with long lost Dad has filled in a nice piece of my treatment puzzle. The goodbye work will make it easier to say hello to life after residential care.

I've thought a lot about the Jay thing. I'm glad I got the opportunity to be a part of the little dude's life. It was hard; I wasn't always sure what to say or do, but man, what an experience. It was important for me to be on the other side; to be the helper instead of the helpee. Besides the boost to self-esteem, it let me see this business from the worker's perspective.

I've always had trouble figuring out why adults work with kids like me. We spit, kick, and swear. We provoke, fight, and yell, "I don't care!"

Why do they do it? I wonder. *Why come in every day?*

Now the answer is clear:
To make a difference.

Six months from now, I'll be home. I'm sure I'll have good and bad days. I'd like to believe that after a horrible day at school, when I was teased for being a group-home kid, a weirdo-

Shit...Hector's face just popped into my head.

Why did he have to die? I miss him.

Why couldn't the world accept a beautiful kid? Prejudice sucks!

I'd like to believe that I'll come home feeling like a piece of dirt...will lie on my bed...replay my crappy day over again...and then try to snap myself out of my funk by thinking about something positive, like what I did for Jay and the Brickmans.

Highland Hills has done a good job with me around the way I think about things. In other words, they've helped me to put the brakes on bad, self-defeating thoughts. To see the light when I'm engulfed in darkness. Sadly, kids like me often view the glass as half-empty. We get so sucked-up in our hopeless-ness that we lack the energy and confidence to move ahead. This place has helped me to look at situations with more hope, and has provided concrete strategies to *snap out* of mind ruts (as I call them).

So, when I'm lying there, feeling like a loser, feel-ing paralyzed to do anything...I'd like to believe that I'll use some of these strategies to get back on track. As I said, I just might think about Jay and the Brick-mans when I'm blue. I know I'll feel better about myself by remembering that there are three people in this world doing a little better because of me. How can you top that?

Hey, I know for a fact, that when Appelstein is having a bad day his mind often conjures up Keyon; he sees that kid braking tackles and dropping run-ning backs like pancakes slapped on a griddle.

You know what? I just figured something out; had me a revelation:

I'm going to work with kids who have been abused when I grow up. I really mean it this time. I know it's a brutal job; the lows must be subterranean, but the highs – yeah, the highs – I bet they can send you to the stars.

Appelstein told me that there are moments in his life when he actually pities people who don't work with kids. He feels bad that they will never experience the indescribably wondrous feelings that spring from your soul when *you know* you've made a difference with a kid. Touch one life and you touch a generation.

Sure, I understand that the highs might not occur as often as the lows; it ain't easy dealing with troubled kids' defenses – all the difficult, rejecting behaviors we exhibit. But think what it would be like if we didn't have them; if nothing existed between the workers and the incredible pain and sadness we kids harbor. Frankly, I don't think many adults could take it. It would hurt too much to see the raw us. Heck, it would hurt us too much. So thank the Lord for defenses.

Well, that's it, pal. I got nothing left. It's time to stop writing and look for babes. I don't know what my future is going to be like. I'm excited and worried. I do know there is no such thing as a bad kid, just bad luck and bad choices.

Every kid is special, and in each and every one of our souls beats the heart of a champion. Make a difference, my friend.

Epilogue

After football season, Keyon reluctantly joined the indoor track team. He would have preferred to lift weights all winter, but his football coach wanted him to do track. So he did track.

He was asked to throw the shot put and high jump. His best jump of the season was six feet even. Not bad for a kid who stands 5 feet, 11 inches, and weighs 190 pounds. Jumping six feet qualified Keyon for the state championship meet – which didn't excite him. Participating in the meet would mean putting off his weight lifting even longer.

Two days after the state championship meet, I called Keyon to talk about the chapter I was writing about him. Before hanging up, I remembered the meet and asked him how he did.

"I won," was his quiet reply.
"You WON!" I screamed.
"Yeah."
"How high did you jump?"
"Six feet, five inches."
"And prior to the meet your best jump ever was six feet even?" I asked incredulously.
"Yeah."

No high school athlete within a six-state radius jumped higher than Keyon this year. But, frankly, I don't think he *jumped* six feet, five inches. I think he *flew* over that that bar. I believe my "little" brother Keyon has been soaring for a long time. I think most kids can – if they believe in their innate power to rise above...

Charlie Appelstein,
A *brother* for life

About the Author

Charlie Appelstein, M.S.W., President of Appelstein Professional Services, provides training, consulting, and literature to psychiatric, residential, foster care, and educational settings throughout the U.S. and Canada. From 1987 to 1993, he served as the Residential Director and Treatment Coordinator for the Nashua Children's Home, a mid-sized residential facility for at-risk kids and their families. In 1991, Charlie won first place honors in the bi-annual Albert E. Trieschman Child Care Literature Competition—essay category, for a paper which has subsequently become *The Gus Chronicles*. His second book, *No Such Thing As a Bad Kid: Understanding and Responding to the Challenging Behavior of Troubled Children and Youth* was published in 1998.

Charlie and his wife and daughter reside in southern New Hampshire. He can be contacted at his business office:

Appelstein Professional Services
12 Martin Avenue
Salem, New Hampshire 03079

charlieap@comcast.net
Website: www.charliea.com

No Such Thing As a Bad Kid

Understanding and Responding to the Challenging Behavior of Troubled Children and Youth

Charlie Appelstein, M.S.W.

Written specifically for teachers, child and youth-care professionals, and foster parents, *No Such Thing As a Bad Kid* is packed with information for *anyone* who lives or works with youngsters at risk. This empowering handbook provides hundreds of hands-on tips and sample dialogues which can help revolutionize your interactions with troubled kids and their interactions with the world. Even parents of children *not* at risk will benefit from this book.

"Anyone concerned with troubled and at-risk youth will be captured by this treasure of practical strategies for respectful behavior management. It is a refreshing new resource."
> – Larry Brendtro
> President
> Reclaiming Children and Youth

"A timely and significant new book that will truly help teachers – at all levels – to better understand and engage their most challenging students."
> – Michelle Booth, Former Executive Director
> Project Alliance, Massachusetts

"Sure to be an instant classic."
> – Dennis Braziel, MSSA, LSW
> Senior Consultant, Child Welfare League of America

About the Publisher

The Gifford School is a private, nonprofit day school with over thirty years of experience providing quality educational and clinical services to students with special academic, behavior, and emotional needs.

The GUS CHRONICLES
Reflections from an Abused Kid

*About: Sexual & Physical Abuse, Residential Treatment,
Foster Care, Family Unification, and Much More*

Charles D. Appelstein, MSW

"By drawing us into his worldview, Gus gives the reader fresh perspectives on what it might be like to live in one of these places we adults call treatment centers. This book will take its place in the training literature ... Textbooks just can't say it like *Gus* does."

Larry Brendtro
President
Recclaiming Children and Youth

"A thoroughly believable account of an abused and troubled youth. Gus's recollections of his first day in residential care were so chillingly similar to mine that I quickly forgot Gus was not real."

John Seita, Ph.D.
Kellogg Youth Initiative Partnerships

Order Form

Quantity		Amount
_____	*No Such Thing As a Bad Kid:* ($19.95)	_____
_____	*The Gus Chronicles I:* ($12.00)	_____
_____	*The Gus Chronicles II:* ($12.00)	_____
	Shipping and handling fee	_____
	10% Discount for orders of 10 books or more (any combination)	– _____
	Total amount enclosed	_____

Shipping and handling costs

1 – 2 books	$2.50 per book
3 – 5 books	$2.00 per book
6 or more books	8% of order

Name _____

Organization _____

Shipping Address _____

City/State/Zip _____

Phone/email _____

Kindly photocopy this order form, fill it out, and mail it, together with your personal check or money order, to:

Appelstein Professional Services (APS)
12 Martin Avenue
Salem, NH 03079
1-603-898-5573
(Phone/Fax)